Better Homes and Gardens®

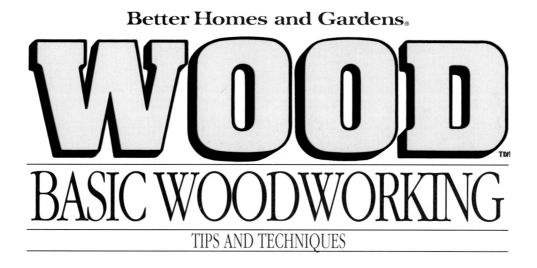

WOOD™
BASIC WOODWORKING
TIPS AND TECHNIQUES

All of us at Meredith® Books are dedicated to giving you the
information and ideas you need to create beautiful and useful
woodworking projects. We guarantee your satisfaction with this
book for as long as you own it. We also welcome your comments
and suggestions. Please write us at Meredith® Books, BB-117,
1100 Walnut St., Des Moines, IA 50309-3400.

A **WOOD** ™ **BOOK**
Published by Meredith® Books

MEREDITH® BOOKS
President, Book Group: Joseph J. Ward
Vice President and Editorial Director: Elizabeth P. Rice
Executive Editor: Connie Schrader
Art Director: Ernest Shelton
Prepress Production Manager: Randall Yontz

WOOD® MAGAZINE
President, Magazine Group: William T. Kerr
Editor: Larry Clayton

BASIC WOODWORKING TIPS AND TECHNIQUES
Produced by Roundtable Press, Inc.
Directors: Susan E. Meyer, Marsha Melnick
Senior Editor: Sue Heinemann
Managing Editor: Ross L. Horowitz
Graphic Designer: Jeff Fitschen
Art Assistant: Ahmad Mallah
Copy Assistant: Amy Handy

For Meredith® Books
Assistant Art Director: Tom Wegner
Technical Adviser: Bill Krier
Contributing Outline Editor: David A. Kirchner

Special thanks to Khristy Benoit

On the front cover: Basic Mortise and Tenon Joinery,
    pages 23–28

Meredith Corporation Corporate Officers:
Chairman of the Executive Committee: E. T. Meredith III
Chairman of the Board, President and Chief Executive Officer:
    Jack D. Rehm
Group Presidents: Joseph J. Ward, Books; William T. Kerr, Magazines;
    Philip A. Jones, Broadcasting; Allen L. Sabbag, Real Estate
Vice Presidents: Leo R. Armatis, Corporate Relations;
    Thomas G. Fisher, General Counsel and Secretary;
    Larry D. Hartsook, Finance; Michael A. Sell, Treasurer;
    Kathleen J. Zehr, Controller and Assistant Secretary

GETTING THE MOST OUT OF YOUR TOOLS

Knowing how to use tools effectively will increase your success at woodworking projects. Learn how routers, scrollsaws, belt sanders, jointers, bench planes, and other tools can do the work for you and save you time.

ROUTER BASICS

Woodworkers love their routers, and it's easy to see why. Few tools can be put to more uses, and none rival the router's ability to quickly and gracefully enhance the appearance of a project. For best results when using your router, keep these tips in mind.

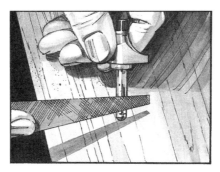

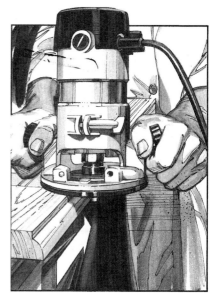

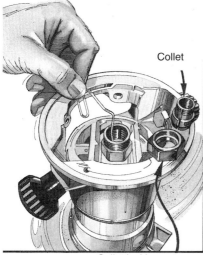

Collet

Collet locking nut

1. First, inspect the collet assembly for resin, wood dust, and other debris that can make bit removal difficult. To avoid sticky situations, start by removing the collet locking nut and collet. Then, blow away any loose debris. With a paper clip, gently scrape any gunk that remains as shown *above* (we removed the router subbase for clarity). Soften stubborn resins with lacquer thinner, then wipe clean.

Note: *Always unplug the router when servicing the collet assembly or changing bits.*

2. One other culprit can make bit removal a hassle: burrs, on the bit shank. Remove them with a few light file strokes as depicted *above*. Now, securely lock the bit in the collet.

3. Before starting your router, always keep these safety pointers in mind:
• Wear eye and lung protection.
• Hold the router comfortably at arm's length and make sure you have enough available power cord to complete the job. If you run out of power cord, the bit will spin too long in one place and could burn the workpiece.
• Walk along with the router as you work, being careful not to overreach or lose your balance.

4. For the best possible cut, move the router along the edges of the surface in a counterclockwise direction as shown *above*. When routing all four edges, cut the end-grain edges first, then cut the edgegrain lengths to minimize edgegrain splinters.

Move the router at a consistent speed, and increase the feed rate if burning occurs. If the grain tears out, take several light passes.

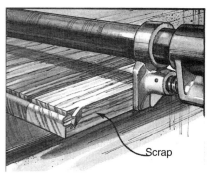

Scrap

5. When routing three edges of a surface, such as a shelf, back the final end-grain cut with scrap to prevent splintering of the workpiece. As shown *above,* the bit chipped out the scrap block, but left the corner of the workpiece crisp and clean.

TEN TIPS FOR IMPROVING YOUR SCROLLWORK

Next time you attend a woodworking show, check out the scrollsaw booths. You'll meet demonstrators who can scroll rings around most woodworkers. What do they know that you may not? Just a few tricks, such as the tips on these pages.

1. Because of the rapid up-down strokes of its arms, a scrollsaw vibrates excessively when not securely fastened to a stand. If your machine doesn't have such a perch, bolt the scrollsaw to a sturdy surface. If you need to store your scrollsaw between uses, clamp it down.

If you can't clamp or bolt down the machine, try placing a thin foam pad, such as a carpet pad, underneath the machine as shown *below*.

2. Scrollsaws come with a variety of blade clamps, but whatever the style, make sure the blade sits straight in the clamps as shown *below.*

With that accomplished, set the blade for the correct tension. Remember that you can tension a wide blade more than a narrow blade and that overtightening will lead to excessive blade breakage. On the other hand, a loose blade will flex sideways and backwards.

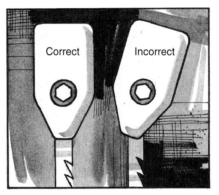

Correct　Incorrect

3. Time flies when you're having fun with a scrollsaw, so adjust the machine's table to a comfortable working height (near elbow level for most people). You'll also find it helpful to sit on a chair or stool.

4. As shown *below,* scrollsaw blades will flex under even slight feed pressure, so you need to occasionally slow down the feed rate and allow the blade to straighten itself. If you don't, you may cut a kerf that's not perpendicular to the table or bowed slightly. While cutting thick or dense stock, you may need to pause every ½" or so.

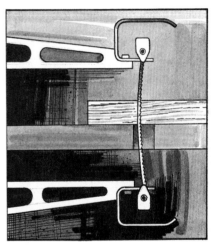

5. We've found that paper patterns are easier to see than patterns transferred directly to the wood surface by carbon paper or other means. Adhere the paper to the workpiece with adhesive spray or double-faced tape.

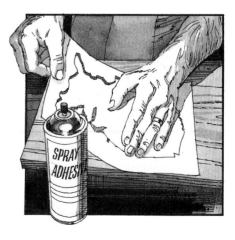

Pad

SPRAY ADHES

6. A dustblower helps you see exactly where you're cutting, but for it to be effective, you must reposition it for each stock thickness. Most blowers put out a small volume of air, so place the hose tip no more than ½" from the cutting action.

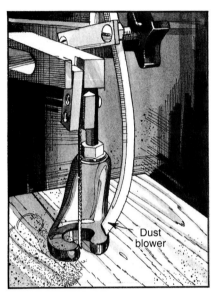

Dust blower

7. As you move the workpiece into the blade, start and exit the cut at a sharp point on the pattern rather than along a smooth line as shown *below*. Otherwise, your lines will have small "humps" where you enter and exit the cut.

8. Because many of us have become accustomed to following layout lines on a bandsaw—a machine that doesn't allow cutting extremely tight curves—we're not used to rotating a workpiece as shown *above*. Experienced scrollers often spin their workpieces in full circles to precisely follow tight twists and turns. When carefully executed, this maneuver may look tricky, but it just requires some practice.

To train yourself, draw some squiggly lines on a scrap piece and see how closely you can follow your markings. Soon you'll be spinning with the best of 'em.

9. Sometimes, you can't spin your way through extremely tight spots such as the narrow corner shown *below center*. To smoothly execute this maneuver, first cut all the way into the corner, then back up the blade for cut 2. Now you have enough room to turn the blade around and make the exit cut.

10. We hear from a lot of readers who have problems cutting thick, hard stock with a scrollsaw. If that sounds like you, try a wider, skip-tooth blade. Go slow and clear away cutting debris by backing the blade out of the cut often.

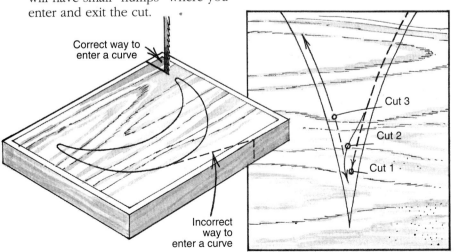

Correct way to enter a curve

Incorrect way to enter a curve

Cut 3

Cut 2

Cut 1

RESAWING THE SAFE AND SIMPLE WAY

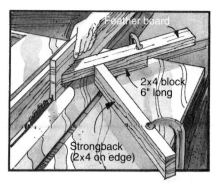

Feather board

2x4 block
6" long

Strongback
(2x4 on edge)

A surprising number of woodworking projects call for thin stock in dimensions such as ⅛", ¼", or ⅜". But that shouldn't pose any problems for you, even if you don't have a thickness planer, or don't want to order the material by mail. Just cut what you need from a thicker piece of stock—normally ¾" or thicker—using your tablesaw and a process called resawing. Here's how:

2. With a try square, check that your blade is set at exactly 90° as shown *above*. Likewise, your fence must be perpendicular to the cutting surface.

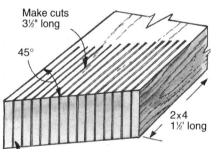

Make cuts
3½" long

45°

2x4
1½' long

Space bandsaw cuts ¼" apart

and positioned just ahead of the blade with all the fingers in contact with the board. We raised the featherboard with a 6"-long block of 2x4 nailed to its underside. Set the strongback, which prevents the featherboard from pivoting toward the rear of the saw, at a 90° angle to the featherboard.

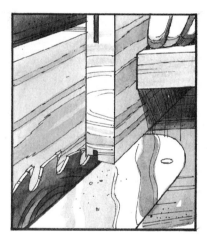

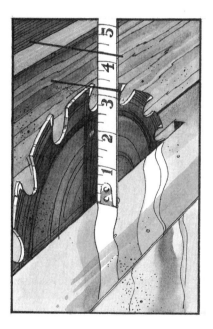

1. To determine how wide a board you can resaw, measure the maximum height of your tablesaw blade as shown *above*. Multiply this measurement times two and subtract ¼" to figure the maximum board width.

Attach an auxiliary ¾" plywood fence to your tablesaw rip fence. Cut the plywood as long as the standard fence and 1" higher than the maximum height of the blade as shown *above*.

3. From a 2x4 that measures 1½–2' long, cut a featherboard as shown *above*. Woodworkers have long used these simple helpers to hold a workpiece safely and securely against their saw's fence.

4. Adjust your fence for the desired thickness of stock. For example, set the fence ¼" from the blade for ¼"-thick stock. Then, clamp the featherboard and another 2'-long piece of 2x4— known as a strongback—to the tablesaw as shown *top right*. The top of the featherboard should be flush with the maximum height of the blade,

5. Before making any cuts, be certain the workpiece has one flat, true face that goes toward the fence. Raise the blade to a height of ¾" for your first cut. Be sure to keep downward pressure on the board with one hand, while feeding the board with a pushstick in your other hand. After completing this cut, flip the board end-for-end, place the same face against the fence, and make a cut into the opposite edge of the board as shown *above*. Repeat this sequence, raising the blade in ½" increments. Be sure to use a sharp, rip-profile blade, and stand to one side of it when sawing.

GET SMOOTH RESULTS FROM YOUR BELT SANDER

A belt sander makes fast work of smoothing down rough stock. But if you're not careful, you can end up with ridges and gouges that seem to take forever to sand away. Here's how to do a perfect job every time.

1. Belt sanders cut aggressively, so you've got to secure the workpiece to the bench before you start. Try this method: Clamp short, narrow stock in a vise, so it projects about ¼" above the clamp jaws.

To secure wide stock, clamp 6"- to 8"-wide plywood stops where shown on the drawing *above*. Again, you want the top surface of the workpiece to project above the stop strips so they don't interfere with the sander.

An alternative method is placing the workpiece on a commercially available rubber pad made just for holding stock for sanding and routing. These ⅛"-thick pads grip the workpiece and prevent it from sliding. You occasionally need to clean dust off the pad by shaking it.

Using a pencil, draw a wavy line across the surface of the stock, as shown on the drawing. This provides you with a visual reference while sanding—after you've completely sanded away the mark, it's time to switch to a finer-grit paper.

2. Starting with 120-grit sandpaper, set the sander on the stock midway between both ends as shown in the drawing *above*. Keep the sander perfectly flat to the wood surface when you turn it on. Hold the sander at a 15° to 20° angle to the direction you're sanding. Belt-sand up and down the length of the stock, moving to the right about 1" at the end of each pass. Let the machine's weight do the work.

3. After you've sanded away the wavy line, switch to a finer-grit belt. Draw a second wavy line, and make straight passes, holding the machine parallel to the grain as shown *above*. Move to the right about 1" after each pass. When the pencil line vanishes again, switch to a finer grit for finish sanding.

4. No matter how carefully you sand, there's always the chance that you'll accidentally gouge the wood. So, each time you finish sanding with a particular grit, check your work before moving to the next grit. We suggest you clamp a small light to your bench, as shown *above*, so that it illuminates the stock from a low angle. By standing behind the light and sighting down the length of the wood, you'll be able to see even the slightest gouges.

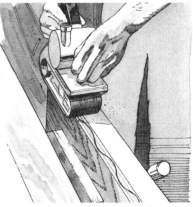

5. Sanding a narrow board or edge can be especially difficult because the sander tends to rock from side to side, rounding over the corners. Here's how to keep the corners sharp: Clamp a piece of scrap, called a *ledger,* to one side of the board (align both surfaces). Make the combined width of the ledger and board approximately equal to the width of the sanding belt. Draw a wavy line on the board and sand it, following the steps *above*.

SQUARING UP STOCK

Despite its gracefully rounded final shape, a cabriole leg must begin with an absolutely square length of wood. That means each face is the same width and forms a 90° angle with adjacent faces. In the cabriole-leg example, a not-quite-square workpiece will yield a slightly distorted leg that's different from the other table or chair legs, even when shaped from the same pattern.

Likewise, square tapered legs, and turned legs with square sections, need to start with squared stock. Here's how to perform this simple— but essential—squaring process, using your jointer and tablesaw.

1. Place the workpiece on a flat surface, such as a saw table, to detect any warp. If the workpiece is bowed, place the hollow side of the bow on your jointer as shown *below.* If you can't detect a bow, place any side onto the jointer Pass the workpiece over the jointer until you have a true, flat surface. In this and the following steps, remove only as much stock as is necessary to true the surface.

2. Set a try square on the outfeed table of your jointer, and carefully adjust the fence to exactly 90°.

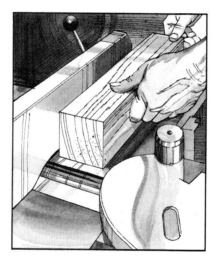

3. Place the trued surface from Step 1 against the jointer fence as shown *above,* and true the adjacent bottom face of the workpiece. Feed the stock slowly for best results.

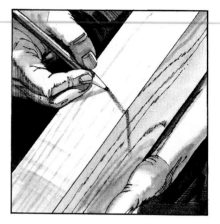

4. With your try square, check the two trued surfaces to make sure that they're at 90° to one another along the entire length of the workpiece. Mark these two surfaces as shown *above* so you don't confuse them with the untrued surfaces.

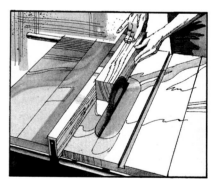

5. Fully raise your tablesaw blade, and check it and the saw's fence for square. Lower the blade so it's ⅛" higher than the workpiece. Hold either trued surface of the workpiece against the fence with the other trued face against the table. Now, adjust the fence for a "skimming" cut. This means that the blade will remove a minimum amount of material and still cut the entire surface. Pass both untrued surfaces through the blade as shown *above.*

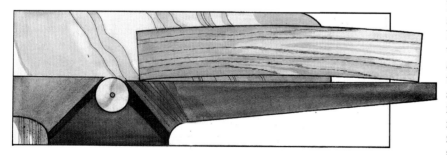

HOW TO SAFELY FEED STOCK THROUGH A JOINTER

In knowledgeable hands, a jointer can make quick work of planing the edges and surfaces of boards. Here's how to get the job done correctly.

1. For most jointer operations, you'll set the fence at 90°. To check this angle, place a try square on the outfeed table as shown *above,* then adjust the fence until daylight disappears between the square's blade and the fence.

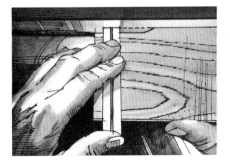

2. Next, make a 1"-long, ⅛"-deep test cut on a piece of scrap stock. Lay the cut edge of the scrap piece against the fence as shown *above,* and check the depth of cut with a rule. Set your depth-of-cut scale according to this test cut.

Direction of feed

3. For a smooth cut, position the workpiece so its grain runs downhill from the outfeed table as shown *above.* If the grain runs every which way, position the board so the majority of the grain flows in the correct direction, take a shallow cut (about ½₂"), and be sure to feed the stock slowly.

4. When jointing edges, hold the surface of the board flat against the fence with your left hand and feed the board with your right hand. Keep your left hand behind the cutterhead as shown in drawing A *right.*

With the board halfway across the cutterhead, swing your left hand around the blade guard as shown in drawing B *right.* Now, place lefthand pressure down onto the outfeed table and toward the fence.

5. To remove stock from surfaces, move your hands in the same motion as described in step 4. To control the workpiece, use the fingertips of your left hand rather than your palm to guide the stock as shown *below.* For stock that's less than 4" wide, use a push block to control the stock with your left

hand. Be sure to clear any dust from the bottom of the block for a good grip.

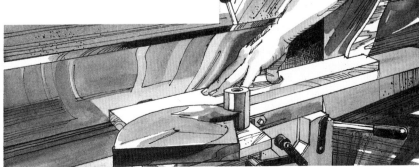

HOW TO INSTALL JOINTER KNIVES

To properly install jointer knives, all you need is a small wooden stick and a little patience. Here's the goof-proof method we use in the *WOOD* magazine shop.

Note: This system works well with jointers that have jackscrews for raising the knives. A few jointers use springs in place of the jackscrews, and with these we advise you to follow the manufacturer's knife-setting instructions. If the machine has no jackscrews or springs for raising the knives, you'll need to use a pair of long magnets to hold the knife edge flush with the outfeed table. Remember to always unplug your jointer before performing any maintenance procedures on it.

1. With a solvent-dampened cloth, clean all pitch and other residue from each knife, gib, and gib bolt (see illustration *below*). Insert all of the parts for one knife into the cutterhead, and adjust the infeed table so it's about ¼" lower than the outfeed table. Tighten the gib bolts just enough to hold the blade and allow the jackscrews still to work.

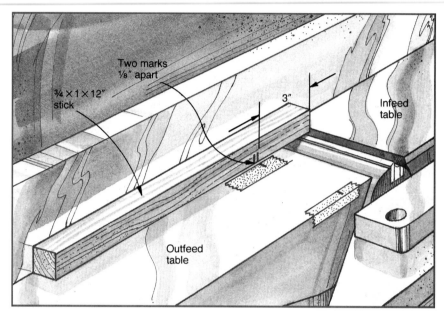

2. Make a ¾x1x12" hardwood stick with at least one trued surface. Using the drawing *above* as your guide, place the trued surface on the outfeed table of your jointer, and mark two lines ⅛" apart and about 3" from the right end of the stick. Rotate the cutterhead so the knife stands straight up, and position the right end of the stick just past the knife. Place two pieces of masking tape on opposite sides of the outfeed table, and mark a line on each of them about 2½" from the knife edge (with the knife still at top center).

3. Rotate the cutterhead counterclockwise so the knife's edge goes clearly below the edge of the outfeed table. With the stick against the jointer's fence, line up the stick's right mark with the mark on the masking tape as shown *below*.

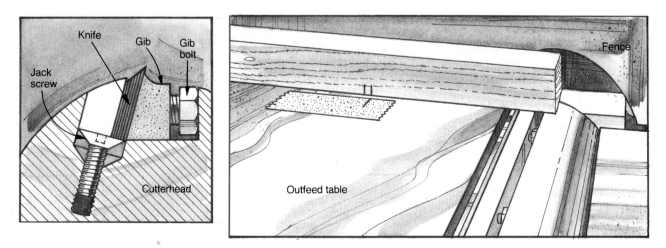

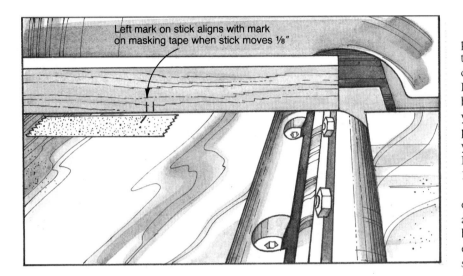

Left mark on stick aligns with mark on masking tape when stick moves ⅛″

6. Now, repeat the previous procedure at the opposite end of the knife. With both ends adjusted correctly, tighten the gib bolts. Recheck the height of the knife at both of its ends. If you're like us, you'll probably have to repeat these procedures several times before you get the knife adjusted properly. Be patient. We've spent as long as 15 minutes on one knife.

Repeat these adjustments for the other knife(s) in the cutterhead. As a final check, joint an edge on two boards and place the edges against each other. This will magnify any sniping at the ends of the boards as shown *below*.

4. Rotate the cutterhead clockwise about a quarter-turn (so the knife travels from the outfeed table toward the infeed table). If you have the knife at the proper height, it will move the stick ⅛″ as shown *above*. If the stick moves *less* than ⅛″, you need to raise the knife. If the stick moves *more* than ⅛″, lower the knife.

5. Raise the far end of the knife to the correct height, gently tighten the gib bolt at the far end, and recheck the knife's height. To make sure that the knife is resting atop the jackscrew, push down on the knife with a softwood block.

To avoid accidentally raising the knife as you tighten the bolt, as shown in the incorrect illustration *below*, try these strategies:

• Grind the jaws of your bolt-tightening wrench as shown *below*.

• Do not slip the jaws of the wrench completely down onto the bolt.

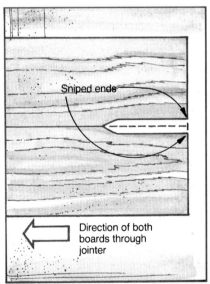

Sniped ends

Direction of both boards through jointer

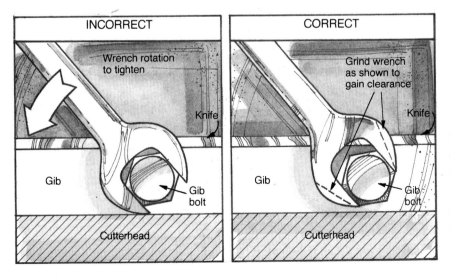

INCORRECT

Wrench rotation to tighten

Knife

Gib

Gib bolt

Cutterhead

CORRECT

Grind wrench as shown to gain clearance

Knife

Gib

Gib bolt

Cutterhead

Sniping results from the knives being too high. Under these circumstances, the jointer knives remove extra material at the end of every pass. If you spot any sniping, and feel that it will cause you to waste too much wood, you'll have to lower the knives.

EDGE-JOINING THE CAN'T MISS WAY

If the world were perfect, you could set your jointer or tablesaw for precisely 90° and end up with flawless butt joints every time as shown in drawing A. Because nothing's perfect, here's a way to set your equipment for about 90° and still cut edges that match exactly as shown in B.

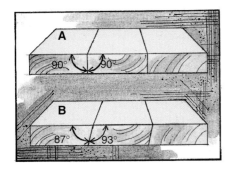

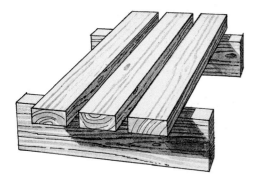

1. Working with nonwarped boards of uniform thickness, place them across a pair of 2x4s so they lie flat and elevated. Then, arrange the boards so that the curvature of their growth rings alternates as shown *above*. This procedure increases the dimensional stability of the glue-up, making it less prone to warping. Now, shuffle the boards around to achieve the best color and grain match, but be careful to maintain the alternating growth-ring pattern for at least 80 percent of the boards.

2. Next, number the boards with a pencil so they stay in proper sequence, and mark alternating Xs and Os along the joint lines on the face sides of the boards as shown *above*. Whether you're using a tablesaw or a jointer to cut the mating edges, these Xs and Os will tell you how to position the boards for ripping and gluing later.

3. If you're cutting the edges with a tablesaw, always place the boards faceup when you trim the O edge as shown *below*. Then, rip the X edge by flipping the board over (face side down with the same end of the board toward you) and ripping it again.

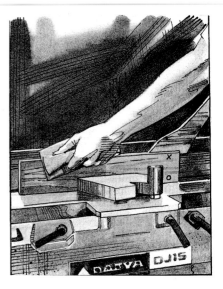

4. This procedure works equally well with a jointer. First, position the board face side out against the fence and pass the O edge through the jointer as shown *above*. Now, place the X edge on the jointer table with the face side (X and O) against the fence and joint that edge. Repeat for the other boards.

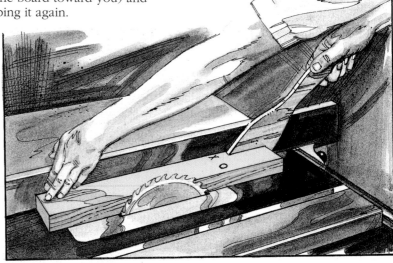

FINE-TUNING YOUR BENCH PLANE

Bench planes have yielded high-quality results for generations of woodworkers, and they still play an important role in the workshop. There's nothing quite like the feel of shaving off a fine ribbon of wood with a properly adjusted bench plane! Here's what you need to do in order to get the results you want (refer to the labeled drawing to identify parts).

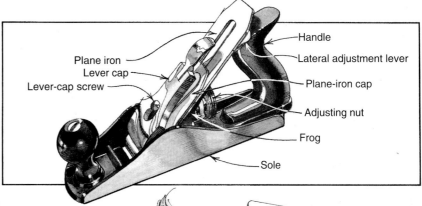

Plane iron
Lever cap
Lever-cap screw
Handle
Lateral adjustment lever
Plane-iron cap
Adjusting nut
Frog
Sole

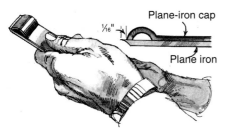

1. First, before making any adjustments, be sure you have a keen, square edge on the plane iron. Regrind and hone the iron if necessary before proceeding.

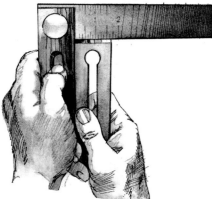

Plane-iron cap
1/16"
Plane iron

2. The plane-iron cap serves as a chip breaker, clearing away material cut by the plane iron. With the bevel of the iron down, slide the cap forward to within about 1/16" of the front of the iron. Soft-grained woods require slightly more reveal. If the entire surface of the cap doesn't seat against the iron, check the cap for square.

3. Fit the cap and iron in place on top of the frog. Now, insert the lever cap and lock it in place. (The lever-cap screw may need adjustment if the cap doesn't snap down smoothly and snugly with reasonable effort.)

Sight down the sole of the plane from the front, and move the lateral adjustment lever until the iron protrudes evenly below the sole. Viewing the blade from the front creates a dark shadow across the blade, making it much easier for you to make the adjustment accurately.

4. The adjusting nut behind the frog regulates the depth of the cut. Again sighting down the sole of the plane from the front, rotate the knob until the iron just barely breaks the plane of the sole. The

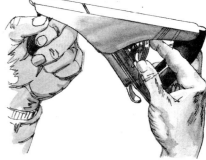

object is to cut a thin, even ribbon of wood with each pass of the plane without any gouging.

5. The real fun begins when you work the plane *with the grain*. With the piece held tightly in a vise and the plane at the angle shown here to avoid fatigue, make your first pass. Listen for a nice "swish." It's an intoxicating sound! If you meet much resistance while planing, retract the blade slightly. And if the shaving is uneven from side to side, adjust the lateral adjustment lever.

HOW TO FOLD AN UNRULY BAND SAW BLADE

No doubt about it! Anyone who has nerve enough can unfold a band saw blade. Just grab it in one hand, remove the ties securing it in its innocent-looking configuration, hold the darn thing out away from you, and watch all the commotion as it gyrates and twists its way to its ready-to-use shape. But folding it again—that's the trick. There are several ways to go about it. Here's one that works particularly well for us.

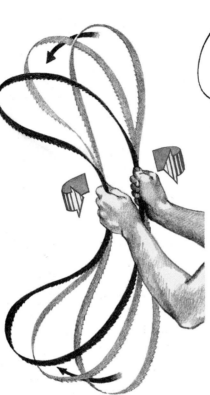

4. You can see here that as the left-hand-over-right-hand action progresses, the blade begins to contort. Don't worry, it's supposed to do that.

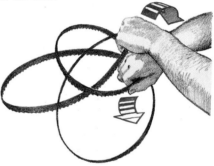

5. At the completion of the motion, the blade "magically" forms a series of rings, which you need to capture quickly with one of your hands. You may have to practice this technique several times to get it down pat, but you'll be the master of your blades in no time at all.

1. Start by grabbing hold of the blade as shown *above*. Two things to keep in mind here: Make sure that the teeth face you and that the loops above and below your hands are about the same size.

2. With your hands about 6" apart, rotate both hands inward (you may notice some discomfort here as the teeth dig into your thumbs—just kidding!). Both ends of the blade will move away from you. If they don't, move your hands closer together and try again.

3. Once you've forced the blade into submission, pass the left hand over the right one. We show you the action in this and the following two sketches, but the whole thing occurs within a matter of seconds.

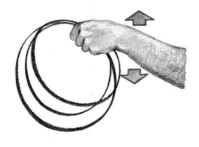

6. Now comes the easy part. Just shake the blade a few times to equalize the size of the rings, bind them together with masking tape, and store.

PUT A SUPER FINE EDGE ON YOUR CARVING TOOLS

Nothing raises the frustration level of a beginning carver more than using dull tools, which make carving dangerous as well as difficult. Carving, however, can be safe and enjoyable if you know how to use the one tool that carvers always keep at arms length—the leather strop.

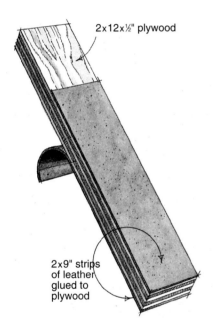

2x12x½" plywood

2x9" strips of leather glued to plywood

1. You can buy a variety of strops, in prices from $15 to $40, but after talking with some prominent carvers, we're convinced that all you need is an easy-to-make two-sided leather strop and two different pastes. You can buy coarse (240 grit) and fine (600 grit) pastes from the source in the Buying Guide at the end of this article.

To make a strop like the one shown *above,* cut a 2×12" piece of ½" plywood, then glue 2×9" strips of belt leather (available from the Buying Guide source) to both sides of the plywood. Attach the leather strips to the same end of the plywood stick to leave a 3" handle at the other end.

2. Now, apply coarse paste to one of the leather strips, and fine paste to the other strip. To sharpen a bench knife, hold the strop (coarse side up) in one hand, and the knife, with its sharp edge facing away from you, in your other hand. Set the blade onto the far end of the strop, with the back edge of the tool just off the leather surface as shown *above.* Press down on the knife and pull it toward you. Now, stroke the opposite side of the blade back down the strop and repeat this step 10–12 times. Then, repeat this process on the fine compound.

3. To sharpen a gouge, hold one end of the tool's edge against the coarse surface of the strop as shown *above.* As you pull the gouge toward you, roll it so all of the cutting edge makes contact with the strop during one stroke. Repeat this stroke 10–12 times. Always pull the gouge toward you—pushing the sharp edge into the leather will cut the strop. Then, flip over the strop and repeat this process on its fine side.

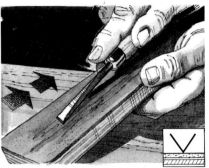

4. Sharpen a V-tool by first stroking one side of the V, then the other on the coarse compound. Next, lay the point of the V on the strop as shown *above,* and pull the tool toward you 5–6 times. Repeat this process on the fine compound.

5. Stripping will form a microscopic burr on the unbeveled (or inside) edge of both the gouge and V-tool. Remove the burr by placing the unbeveled edge of the tool along the corner of the strop as shown *above.* Then, pull the tool toward you 3 times and repeat this process on the other side of the strop.

Buying Guide
• **Belt leather.** 2×44" strip. For current prices visit your local Tandy Leather dealer or contact Tandy Leather Co., PO Box 791, Dept. WO289, Fort Worth, TX 76101.
• **600 grit compound.** Item No. 09L81, and 240 grit, item No. 09L82. For current prices contact Woodcraft, 210 Wood County Industrial Park, PO Box 1686, Parkersburg, WV 26102-1686. (800/535-4486).

HOW TO PROPERLY TIGHTEN HANDSCREW CLAMPS

Handscrew clamps have several things going for them. First, unlike any other clamp, they can easily clamp parts that meet at odd angles. Second, they provide greater reach than most metal clamps. And if that weren't enough, they tend not to crawl or mar project surfaces when they're tightened.

Handscrew clamps are produced in a dozen sizes. Maximum jaw openings range from 2" to 17" and reach (the distance from the front spindle to the jaw end) varies from 2" to 12". The hard maple jaws and cold-drawn steel screws last a lifetime, and have outlived many a woodworker.

If you have never used a handscrew clamp, figuring out how to properly tighten one can be perplexing. But like most everything else, it's not hard once you know how to do it.

Clamping parallel surfaces

Start by making sure the jaws run parallel to each other. The best way to do this is to start with the jaws closed. Also, always hold the clamp the same way—grasp the rear handle in your right hand and the front handle in your left. With the clamp in hand, extend your arms,

and imagine that the clamp handles are pedals on a bicycle. To close the jaws, "pedal" forward, rotating your wrists to spin the handscrew clamp around. To open the jaws, "pedal" backward.

When clamping an object, adjust the jaws until they are slightly wider than the item being clamped, then position the handscrew clamp with the front spindle as close to the work as possible.

With the jaws parallel to each other, and just slightly wider than the object being clamped, close the front spindle until it is finger-tight on the object, as shown in photo A.

Now, grasp the front spindle handle and tighten it another ⅛

of a turn, as shown in photo B.

Apply final pressure to the object being clamped by tightening the handle on the rear spindle as shown in photo C. (The jaws of the handscrew clamp must sit flush on the workpiece to distribute pressure evenly along the length of the jaws.) Closely eyeball the mating to check for continuous contact between the clamped project and the maple jaws. Light peeking through either near the jaw end or the front spindle indicates uneven pressure and may require adjustment or reclamping. It only takes a few practice clampings to get the "swing" of these versatile clamps.

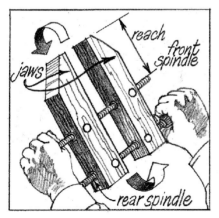

A

B

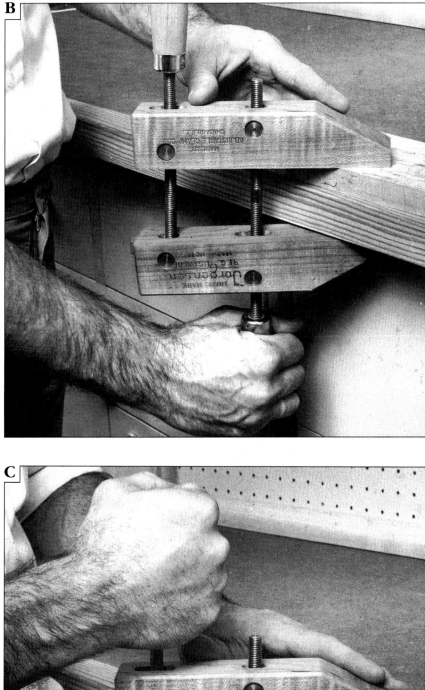

Clamping projects at an angle

The goal remains the same when you clamp irregular objects: to bring as much of the jaw surface as possible in contact with the project being clamped.

Start by "pedaling backwards" to open the jaws. Turn either the front or rear handle to make the jaw ends come together or move apart at an angle. Adjust this angle to match the object being clamped (see photo D). Place the clamp on the object and tighten either the front or rear spindle for continuous contact between both jaws and the clamped object. If "slippery" glue causes the pieces to slide, separate them and let the glue get a little more tacky before clamping.

D

C

THE PERFECT HINGE MORTISE

Hand-cutting mortises (gains) for hinges can be tedious work, especially if your project has lots of doors. Worse yet, one little slip and you end up with an ill-fitting hinge. Here's how to speed things along—and end up with a perfect fit every time.

1. Separate the hinge leaves (if possible) and cut a piece of double-faced tape for each. The tape helps you accurately position the leaf, and holds it securely in place for step 2.

2. Tape the hinge leaf in position, drill pilot holes, and screw the leaf to the surface. This way, the leaf won't slip when you mark the hinge mortise and drill the pilot holes. To avoid damaging the heads of finish screws, use surplus screws of the same size.

3. Carefully score end and side cuts with a sharp knife. Scoring gives you more precise lines than you'll get with a pencil. It also helps ensure that your initial cuts won't split the wood fibers along the grain.

4. Back out the screws and remove the leaf. Mark the mortise's depth. Holding your chisel perfectly vertical with its bevel facing the inside of the mortise, make stop cuts at the ends and side. Easy does it. Don't try to cut to the full depth in one operation, lest you score too deeply and overshoot your mark.

Next make a series of crosswise depth cuts along the length of the mortise—the more cuts, the better.

5. Holding the chisel at a low angle to the wood, bevel side down, clean out the hinge mortise. Work from the center toward the ends. After you've made these lifting cuts, check the depth of the leaf in the mortise. Repeat steps 4 and 5 until the leaf lies about 1/32" above the surrounding surface.

6. Holding the chisel bevel side up, make light, flat paring cuts across the width of the mortise to achieve a perfectly smooth, flat bottom. When you're done, the leaf face should be perfectly flush with the surface.

HOW TO CREATE MADE-TO-MATCH CABINET PANELS

Eye-catching cabinet panels that match each other in a cathedral or "V" pattern don't happen by accident. Such results require simple, upfront planning. What's the trick? To begin with, you need to construct the panel from two or more boards. Here's how to go about it.

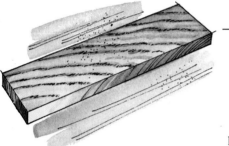

1. Select boards with relatively straight grain lines that run diagonally from edge to edge such as the one shown in the illustration *above*.

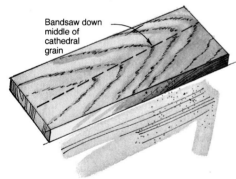

2. If you can't find enough of these boards, you may have to make your own from other boards. For example, you could use a cathedral-grained board such as the one shown *above* and bandsaw it down the middle of the cathedral pattern. Then, straighten the bandsawed edges on a jointer to get two usable boards with diagonal grain.

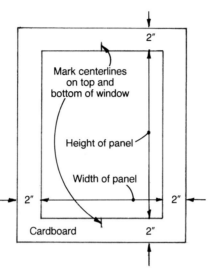

3. Now, cut out a window in a piece of cardboard or hardboard to the dimensions of your panel as shown *above*. Allow a 2" border around the window, and mark centerlines at the top and bottom.

4. Place the window over an attractive portion of the stock, and align the window centerlines with the edge of the workpiece. Mark the board (with a pencil) along the outside edges of the window. See illustration *above*. Crosscut the board along these lines.

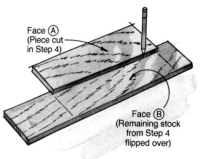

5. Flip over the remaining piece(s) of stock, and slide one of these pieces along the edge of the trimmed board to find the best grain match. You may have to overlap the trimmed board on the other board and angle it as shown *above* to symmetrically match up the cathedral peaks. With the match made, mark the untrimmed board for length. If you need to overlap the untrimmed piece, mark on the top face of the bottom board, running a pencil along the edge of the trimmed board. ·

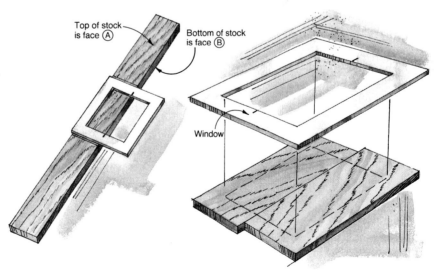

6. Apply glue and edge-join the two pieces of stock. Then, place the window frame over this workpiece, positioning it for the best appearance. Mark the panel location along the inside edges of the frame. Cut the panel to size.

PROJECT-BUILDING FUNDAMENTALS

Making a mortise and tenon joint, constructing a cabinet, creating a perfect miter joint, and crafting dovetailed drawers all become relatively simple once you know the fundamentals. To help you with chairs, tables, bookcases, shelves, and other projects, there are woodworkers' standards for you to follow.

BASIC MORTISE AND TENON JOINERY

Our mortising jig and a plunge router make the going easier and more accurate than ever before.

For some reason, the words "mortise and tenon" scare lots of woodworkers. Many hobbyists assume that only true craftsmen have the skills necessary to master this superstrong joint. Not so! Anyone willing to invest the time it takes to read this article, and make the mortising jig we have developed, can fashion good-looking, tight-fitting joints the first time out.

While many variations of the mortise and tenon exist, getting into all of them at the outset will only confuse you. That's why we decided to concentrate on the basics. We'll use a simple frame with hidden mortise and tenon joints as the example, but the information we present applies to other situations as well.

Before reading on, you may find it helpful to study the sketch on page 24 *top.* It will familiarize you with the terminology we'll be using later on. It also gives you some standard sizing information for mortises and tenons.

Note: If you want to know how to lay out mortise and tenon joints for raised panel doors or for joining the legs and aprons of tables (or the legs and rails of chairs), see page 29.

Cutting the frame members to size

After determining the finished size of the frame you want to construct, cut the stiles and rails to size. Don't forget to factor the length of the tenons into the length of the rails. Cut an extra rail, too— it will serve as a layout template.

Laying out the mortises and tenons

You'll be handling the various frame members a lot during and after layout. So, to avoid confusion (not to mention cutting errors), start by carefully laying them out, faceup, as they will be

when assembled. Then, number each joint with a pencil, identify the outside edge of each member, and mark the inside edge of each rail on both ends of each stile, as shown, *below left.*

Now, make yourself a layout template, using the extra rail you cut earlier. First lay out any rabbets, grooves, or profiles you plan to cut into the frame members. Then, using a square, mark the length of the tenons on the template as shown, *below center.* Remember that the length of hidden tenons typically equals ⅔ the width of the mortised frame members.

Next, with a marking gauge, lay out all four of the tenon's borders on the template where shown in the sketch, *below right.* You may want to refer to the anatomy drawing on page 24, *top,* and review the standards presented there.

Once you've marked the template, use it and the marking gauge to transfer all of the lines

continued

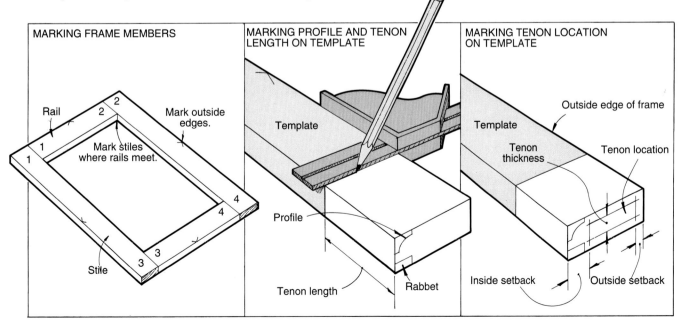

MARKING FRAME MEMBERS

Rail
Mark outside edges.
Mark stiles where rails meet.
Stile

MARKING PROFILE AND TENON LENGTH ON TEMPLATE

Template
Profile
Tenon length
Rabbet

MARKING TENON LOCATION ON TEMPLATE

Template
Tenon thickness
Outside edge of frame
Tenon location
Inside setback
Outside setback

BASIC MORTISE AND TENON JOINERY
continued

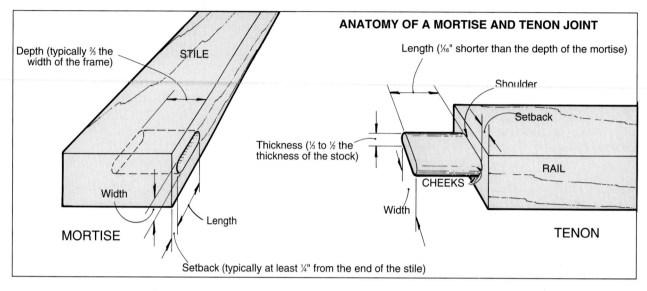

ANATOMY OF A MORTISE AND TENON JOINT

Depth (typically ⅔ the width of the frame)

STILE

Length (1/16" shorter than the depth of the mortise)

Shoulder

Setback

Thickness (⅓ to ½ the thickness of the stock)

RAIL

Width

CHEEKS

Width

Length

MORTISE

Setback (typically at least ¼" from the end of the stile)

TENON

LAYOUT SEQUENCE

SETTING THE MARKING GAUGE	MARKING THE TENONS	MARKING THE MORTISES

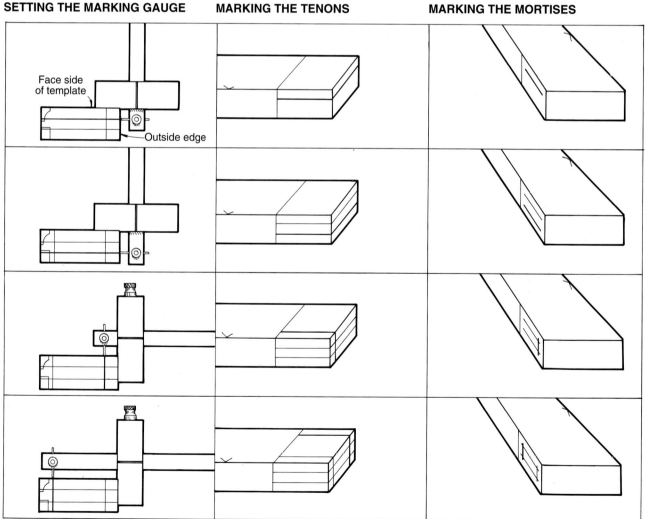

Face side of template

Outside edge

from the template onto the frame members. The series of sketches on the following page shows you the progression we use to do the layout work. Note that once we set the marking gauge each step of the way, we mark both the mortise and tenon on all of the rails and stiles before changing the setting. Doing this ensures that the mortises and tenons will be mirror images of each other. Note also that we set the gauge from the face side of the template for both lines that define the thickness of the tenons. This is just in case the members vary slightly in thickness.

Cutting the mortises

1. Start by securing the jig in a vise. Then, fit one of the stiles in the jig, and position and clamp the fence so that the stile fits snugly against the alignment blocks.

Note: *Always check to be sure that the face side of the piece being mortised is against the jig. Doing this ensures that the face side of frame members will be flush with each other*

2. Slide one end of the stile toward the center of the jig, and clamp it there with the hold-down clamp. Now, loosen the wing nuts holding the router base in place, and carefully center the router bit over the mortise. Retighten the wing nuts. Don't worry too much about the router base being exactly perpendicular to the jig; it needn't be.

3. To limit the travel of the router, line up the bit with each end of the mortise and set the stop collars with an allen wrench.

4. To ensure consistent placement of succeeding mortises, clamp a stop block to the jig. Be sure to snug the block up against the end of the material.

5. When setting the depth of cut, keep in mind that you want the mortise to be approximately 1/16" deeper than the length of the tenon. This extra depth forms a reservoir for glue that will be forced to the bottom of the mortise during glue-up. If you don't provide space for the glue to build up, even with heavy clamp pressure you may not be able to bring the stiles and rails completely together to form a tight joint.

6. It's best to make several shallow passes with the router when cutting the mortises. We generally move down in 1/4" increments. When you've reached the bottom, make another plunge at both ends of the mortise to remove any minor irregularities that may be left from previous cuts. When you're finished with the first mortise, remove the stile and insert the other one, again making absolutely sure that the face side rests against the jig.

7. To cut the mortises at the other end of the stiles, you need to
continued

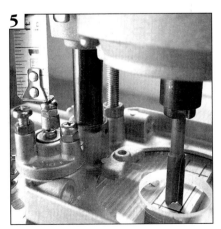

BASIC MORTISE AND TENON JOINERY

continued

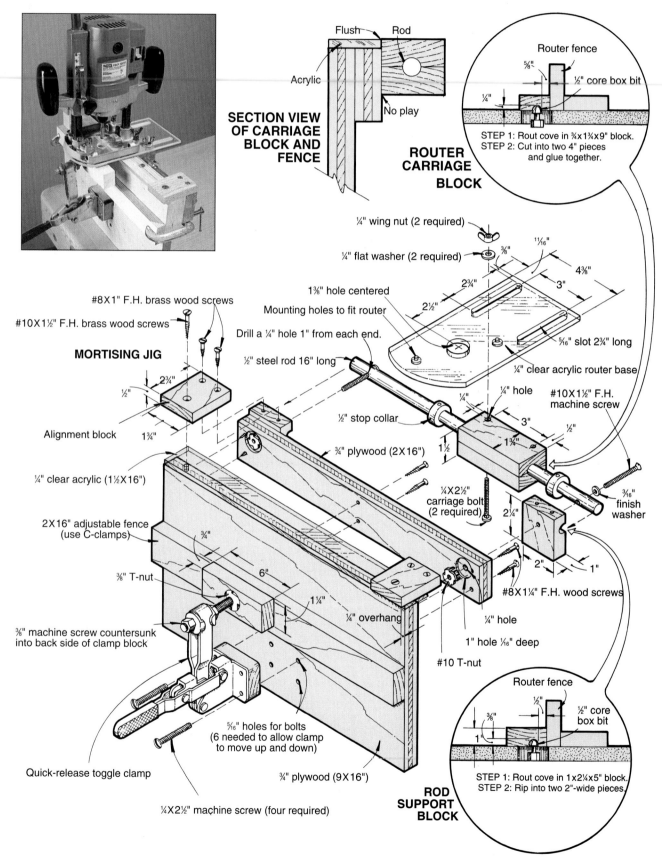

Flush
Rod
Acrylic
No play

SECTION VIEW OF CARRIAGE BLOCK AND FENCE

Router fence
⅝"
½" core box bit
¼"

STEP 1: Rout cove in ¾x1¾x9" block.
STEP 2: Cut into two 4" pieces and glue together.

ROUTER CARRIAGE BLOCK

¼" wing nut (2 required)

¼" flat washer (2 required)

1⅜" hole centered

Mounting holes to fit router

Drill a ¼" hole 1" from each end.

3/8"
11/16"
4⅜"
2¾"
2½"
3"
5/16" slot 2¾" long
¼" clear acrylic router base

#8X1" F.H. brass wood screws

#10X1½" F.H. brass wood screws

MORTISING JIG

2¾"
½"
1¾"

Alignment block

½" steel rod 16" long

½" stop collar

¼" hole
¼" hole
#10X1½" F.H. machine screw
3"
½"

¼" clear acrylic (1½X16")

¾" plywood (2X16")

1½

1¾"

#10X1½" F.H. machine screw

3/16" finish washer

2X16" adjustable fence (use C-clamps)

¾"

¼X2½" carriage bolt (2 required)

2¼"

⅜" T-nut

6"

1¼"

¼" overhang

2"
1"

⅜" machine screw countersunk into back side of clamp block

#8X1¼" F.H. wood screws

¼" hole

1" hole 1/16" deep

#10 T-nut

5/16" holes for bolts (6 needed to allow clamp to move up and down)

Quick-release toggle clamp

¾" plywood (9X16")

Router fence
½"
⅜"
½" core box bit
1"

STEP 1: Rout cove in 1x2¼x5" block.
STEP 2: Rip into two 2"-wide pieces.

ROD SUPPORT BLOCK

¼X2½" machine screw (four required)

move the stop block to the other side of the router bit. To position it correctly, first slide the router to the right until it makes contact with the stop collar. Then, insert one of the stiles into the jig, face side in, carefully aligning the router bit with the right-hand end of the mortise, and clamp the stock in place. Now, clamp the stop block against the end of the stile, and cut the remaining mortises as before.

Cutting the tenons

1. Place one of the stiles face side down, on your table saw, and set the height of the blade, using the mortise as a guide.

2. Now, using your layout template, set the rip fence to control the tenon length. To ensure that the template is perpendicular to the rip fence, hold the template against the miter gauge.

3. To test the blade height setting, position your layout template, facedown, on the table saw, and make one pass at the end of it. Then check it against one of the mortises as shown. Make any necessary adjustments.

4. Remove the material from the *face side* of each end of each rail. You will notice some saw marks left by the dado blade, but don't

worry about them. The tenons needn't be smooth.

5. Again using your template, this time with the *back side facing down,* cut away a portion of the material from its back side. Now, check the fit of the tenon in one of the mortises. You want a snug, but not a tight, fit. Raise or lower the blade to adjust the thickness of the

tenon, if necessary, then remove the material from the back side of each end of each rail.

6. To remove the material from the outside and inside setback portions of the tenons, turn once again to your trusty template, elevate the blade to the proper height for each setback, make test

continued

Our mortising jig: it does the job quickly and accurately

As you probably know, there are several ways to cut mortises, both by hand and with machines. Cutting mortises by hand has always seemed too labor-intensive to us, especially if we have lots of them to make. And while you can purchase a mortising attachment for your drill press, if you have one, we think our jig is faster and more accurate.

The Exploded View Drawing and the detail drawings that accompany it *(opposite page)* give you the information you

need to build the jig. And on page 25 we show you how to set it up and use it.

Note: The jig does require that you have a plunge router to make the cuts. If you don't have one already, we think the money you spend on this versatile tool will be well worth it. It not only makes cutting mortises a snap, you can also put it to good use for cutting stopped dadoes and grooves, template routing, and many other cutting chores. Several router manufacturers have one or more plunge models

in their line. Also, you'll need a long-shanked, carbide-tipped straight router bit.

Buying Guide
• **Quick-release toggle clamp.** Catalog no. 173-003. For current prices contact Woodworker's Supply, 5604 Alameda, NE, Albuquerque, NM 87113 (505/821-0500).

• **Stop collars.** ½" set collars. Stock no. S/C ½. For current prices contact Standard Bearings, PO Box 823, Des Moines, IA 50304 (515/265-5261).

BASIC MORTISE AND TENON JOINERY
continued

cuts on your template, check them against the mortise, and remove the remaining material.

7. To round off the corners of each of the tenons, we use a sanding belt wrapped around a piece of plywood. With it, we chamfer each corner and round it over slightly. Take care not to sand the top and bottom cheeks of the tenons, though. By doing so, you can cause distortion of the frame members. Also be sure to hold the sanding block square to the tenon.

Accidentally beveling the tenons will weaken the mechanical strength of the joint.

8. After rounding the corners, you'll still need to remove some material at the base of the tenons. Otherwise, you'll find that the joints won't close all the way. We use a chisel to remove the excess material.

Gluing and clamping the frame

If you've made all of your cuts carefully, this part of the project

should be a piece of cake. It's a good idea to dry-clamp the frame to make sure that the members fit together tightly and that the face sides of the frame members are flush.

If everything checks out, apply glue to both the tenons and the mortises, assemble the frame, and clamp until the glue sets up. Be sure to check the frame for square while the glue is still wet.

5

6

7

8

BASIC CABINET CONSTRUCTION

Woodworkers everywhere appreciate the beauty of well-crafted cabinetry. But many of these same people labor under a false impression—that cabinets must be terribly difficult to make. Not so! And to prove it, we're going to walk you through the steps that will yield good-looking cabinets every time.

We've selected a straightforward example—a base cabinet with a bar sink and a matching wall cabinet—to illustrate the basics you need to know as a novice cabinetmaker. (See the Exploded View drawings *below* for how they go together.) Once you've mastered the procedures that follow, you can handle many cabinetmaking situations. Though the dimensions, and maybe even the style of

continued

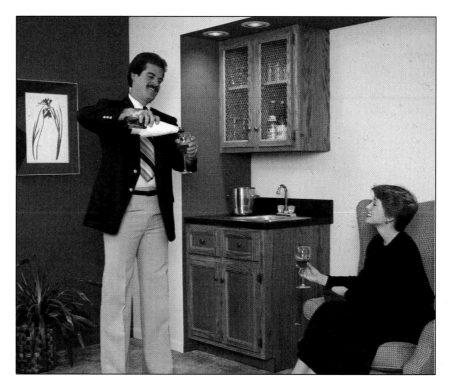

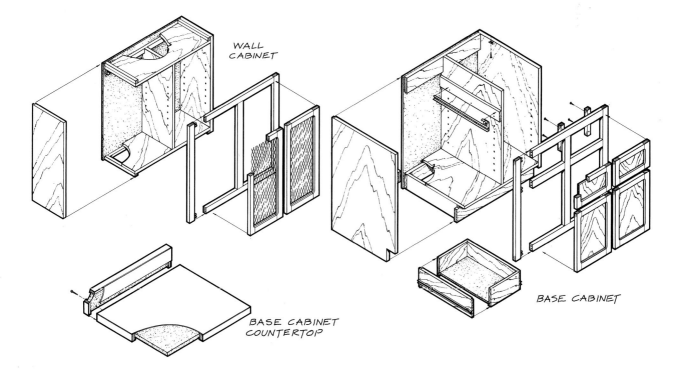

WALL CABINET

BASE CABINET COUNTERTOP

BASE CABINET

BASIC CABINET CONSTRUCTION
continued

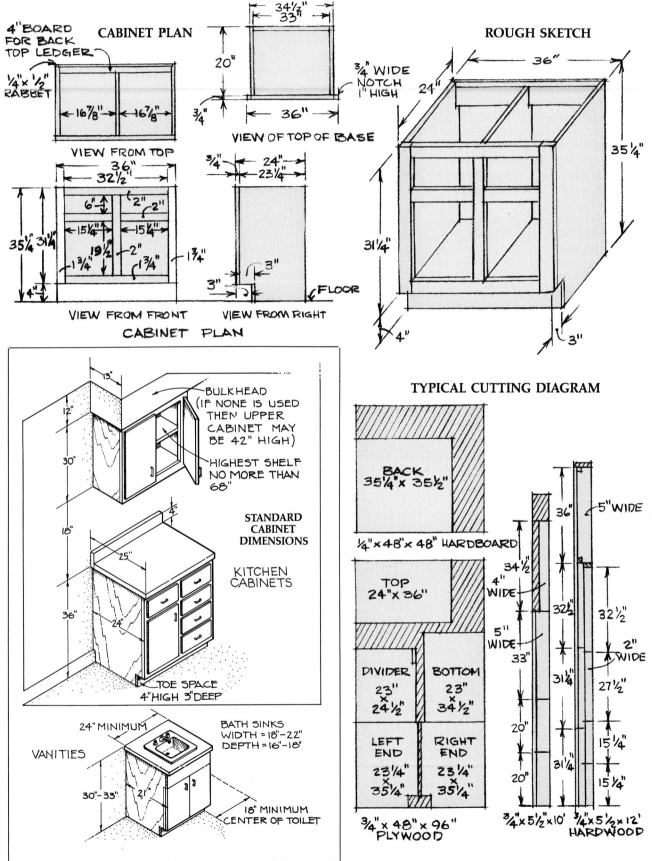

CABINET PLAN

4"BOARD FOR BACK TOP LEDGER

¼"x ½" RABBET

16⅞"   16⅞"

VIEW FROM TOP

34½"
33"

20"

¾"

36"

VIEW OF TOP OF BASE

¾" WIDE NOTCH 1" HIGH

ROUGH SKETCH

36"

21"

35¼"

31¼"

4"   3"

36"
32½"

6"   2"—2"

15¼"   15¼"

35¼" 31¼"   19½"   2"
1¾"   1¾"   1¾"

4"

VIEW FROM FRONT

¾"   24"
23¼"

3"   3"

3"

FLOOR

VIEW FROM RIGHT

CABINET PLAN

13"

12"

30"

BULKHEAD (IF NONE IS USED THEN UPPER CABINET MAY BE 42" HIGH)

HIGHEST SHELF NO MORE THAN 68"

STANDARD CABINET DIMENSIONS

KITCHEN CABINETS

4"

25"

18"

36"

24"

TOE SPACE 4" HIGH 3" DEEP

24" MINIMUM

VANITIES

BATH SINKS WIDTH = 18"-22" DEPTH = 16"-18"

30"-33"   21"

18" MINIMUM CENTER OF TOILET

TYPICAL CUTTING DIAGRAM

BACK 35¼" x 35½"

¼"x 48"x 48" HARDBOARD

TOP 24"x 36"

DIVIDER 23" x 24½"

BOTTOM 23" x 34½"

LEFT END 23¼" x 35¼"

RIGHT END 23¼" x 35¼"

¾" x 48" x 96" PLYWOOD

36"   5"WIDE

34½"

4" WIDE   32½"   32½"

5" WIDE   2" WIDE

33"   31¼"   27½"

20"   15¼"

31¼"   15¼"

20"

¾"x 5½"x10'   ¾"x5½"x12' HARDWOOD

cabinet, may change, much of what you learn will still apply.

Start with a plan

Obviously, before you order a single sheet of plywood or a board for your project, you have to have a good idea of how you want the end product to look. You'll also want to settle on the cabinets' overall dimensions.

The rough sketch

Though some visually oriented woodworkers can build as they go, most of us need a rough sketch to guide us along the way. This sketch needn't be sophisticated (see our example in the shaded area *opposite*), but do try to be as detailed as possible. It's also helpful to draw front, end, and top views of the project as well as any other details that clarify construction. Since there are some cabinetmaking standards often used by professionals that you may not know about, we've included them in the box *opposite*. Use them to flesh out your rough sketch.

The story pole and how it can help you

Once you have established the width, depth, and height of a cabinet, make yourself a *story pole.* This device, which can be a scrap piece of lumber or sheet goods, will show you *exactly* how much room the cabinet will occupy when it's finished. It also shows you where various members of the cabinet will be located. And most important, a story pole allows you

Visualizing with story pole.

to measure distances exactly.

The photo at *the bottom of the previous column* shows what information we transfer to the front side of the story pole and how we use it to visualize the end result. (Essentially, what we have here is a section view of the cabinet near the front.) After studying the story pole and making any desired

A view from the top

adjustments, we then turn our scrap board over and plot what amounts to a top view of the cabinet (see the photo *above*). If you want, you can use the same technique to take a look at the cabinet's depth.

Make a cutting diagram

When you make a cutting diagram, you're doing yourself a couple of big favors. Not only does the diagram help you figure the materials requirements for the cabinet, it also serves as a guide when it comes time to cut out the components.

Note: *When laying out the cabinet's end panels on the plywood, make sure that you have the grain running from top to bottom. The same applies to doors if you plan to use plywood for them.*

How to build a base cabinet carcass

The base of a base cabinet adds structural support at the bottom of the cabinet. It also helps form the toe kick, the strategically placed recess at the front of the cabinet that allows you to get close to the cabinet without kicking it.

Toe kicks typically measure 4" high X 3" deep when the cabinet is finished. But since the bottom of the cabinet sits on the base and the top edge of the bottom face frame

rail rests flush with the bottom's top edge, you have to make the base somewhat taller to end up with a 4" high toe kick. (After referring to our story pole, we cut the *toe board* 5" high and as long as the cabinet is wide.)

Now, lay the toe board on a flat surface and mark the location of the notches that the end panels will pass through. Also lay out the position of the end panels as shown *below*. (The notch at both ends of the toe board in this instance measures ¾" wide and 1" deep.)

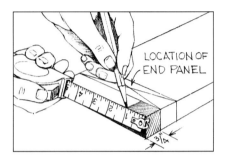

LOCATION OF END PANEL

After notching the toe board, cut the sides and the back of the base to size. Since neither the sides nor back will show when you complete the cabinet, you may want to use scrap wood for these parts.

After dry-fitting the parts, nail and glue scrap wood cleats ¾" in from each end of the back and 1½" in from each end of the toe board. Then, glue and nail the base together as shown in the photo below. Note that the cleats make aligning and nailing together the base pieces a very easy procedure.

While the glue is still wet, check for square by measuring diagonally from corner to corner as shown in the first photo on page 32. (If the measurements differ, your base isn't *continued*

Assembling the cabinet's base

BASIC CABINET CONSTRUCTION
continued

Checking for square

square.) To square the base, you'll have to *rack* it as shown in the photo below. (You may have to make several adjustments to get the base into square, so be patient.)

To hold the base in square, nail braces across the corners as shown in the photo *below*.

Racking the base

Cut the end panels

Typically, end panels measure ¾" shorter than the finished height of the cabinet and ¾" narrower than the depth of the cabinet. Start by cutting the side panels to size. Then, fasten the panels together (good faces out) with cleats tacked to two adjacent edges. The cleats keep the panels in alignment while you cut their notches.

Mark the location of the 4"-high x 3"-deep notch on both panels. If you'll be using a table saw, you have to make sure not to cut too far when making your cuts. To do this, raise the blade to its highest setting and mark the point on the auxiliary fence at which the blade enters the work.

Set the fence the correct distance from the blade, test the measurement on scrap, and then make your first cut (stop the blade when your

cutoff mark aligns with the one on the fence). Now, turn the panels over, reset the rip fence, and make the second cut.

You'll notice that the cuts fall somewhat short of the cutoff marks. Finish them with a handsaw, as shown in the photo *below*. Before separating the panels, make a mark on the face of each (doing

Notching the end panels

this will enable you to identify the outside of the panels later).

To complete the machining of the cabinet end panels, you need to cut a ½" rabbet ¼" deep along the back edge of the panels. Unless you have a dado set or blade, making the rabbet requires two cuts. We show the setup for the first pass *below*. Note that a feather board and a brace (both clamped to the saw table) provide the necessary control to make the cut accurately. To make the second cut, reset the rip fence, and the height of the saw blade, make a test cut, then complete the rabbet.

Rabbeting the end panels

Cut and install the bottom, back, and divider

Start by dry-fitting the end panels and the base. Pipe clamps will hold the assembly together well enough

Measuring depth of bottom

to take your measurements. Measure for the depth of the bottom as shown in the photo *above* (note that the bottom aligns with the front of the end panels and the rabbet in back). Measure again for the width of the bottom, then cut the bottom to size. (Since the divider panel is the same depth as the bottom, cut both parts using the same saw setting.)

Set the bottom on the base, then measure the height of the divider panel as shown in the photo *below*. Cut the divider to size.

Measure and cut the ¼" hardboard cabinet back and the cleat that joins the end panels at the top back of the cabinet. (We

Determining height of divider

used a 5"-wide cleat.) Then, glue and nail the end panels and bottom

Securing cleat to end panels

to the base. Secure the cleat between the end panels, either using hot-melt glue as we did here, or with glue and clamps.

Predrill the hardboard back, then screw it to the end panels, base, and top cleat. Slip the divider into position and mark the bottom of the notch you need to cut in its top back edge (see the photo *below).* Notch and install the divider in its

Marking notch in divider

correct location. (Refer to your story pole for the exact location of the divider.)

How to build a wall cabinet carcass

Though base and wall cabinets do share many construction similarities, they differ in several respects, too. That's why we feel it's necessary to take you quickly through the following wall-cabinet carcass how-to.

Begin by cutting the end panels to size (refer to your story pole or drawing for the correct size). Then, cut a ½" rabbet ¼" deep along the back edge of the panels.

Now, cut ¾"x¾" hardwood cleats, and glue and screw them to the top and bottom of the end panels as shown in the photo *below.* After doing this, rip the top and bottom to the correct width, then crosscut them to the correct length.

Glue and screw the top and bottom to the cleats on the end

Fastening cleats to end panels

Measuring height of divider

panels, check for square, and allow the glue to dry. Then, measure as shown in the photo *above* to determine the correct height of the divider panel. (Note that we took the measurement near the end panel. By doing this, we avoided getting an inaccurate measurement if the top or bottom panel had been bowed.) Cut the divider panel to size.

To add further stability to the cabinet, cut and install hardwood ledgers below the top and bottom shelves. (We used a ¾"x¾" ledger under the bottom shelf and a ¾"x 1½" one under the top.)

Now, cut, notch, and install the plywood divider, and cut the back to size and screw it to the carcass.

Build the face frame

Face frames tie the front of the cabinet together structurally and at the same time finish it off visually. When determining how wide to cut the various face frame members, keep in mind that you want it to look balanced when you complete the cabinet.

In the base cabinet we're using as our example, the stiles and the bottom rail measure 1¾" wide; the top rail, mullion (or vertical member between the stiles), and muntins (the horizontal members between the rails), 2". Why the difference? All parts in the latter grouping have two doors or drawers overlapping them, whereas the stiles and the bottom rail have only one doing so. The net result: a visually balanced frame.

Keep in mind, too, that whenever you cut face frame parts, you do so from the outside in: stiles first, then the rails, then the

mullion, and the muntins. But when you assemble the frame, you do so from the inside out: muntins first, and so on.

Start by measuring the distance between the top of the cabinet carcass and the top surface of the cabinet's bottom. We added 1¾" (the width of the bottom rail) to this measurement to determine the length of the stiles.) Cut the stiles to length.

To figure the length of the rails, measure from the outside of one of the end panels to the outside of the other. Add ¼" to that figure, then subtract the combined widths of the stiles. Cut the rails to size.

The photo *below* shows a quick, easy way to make sure the rails are the right length. Set up a length stop, position the rail against it, and move the miter gauge forward just far enough to nick the rail. Pull the

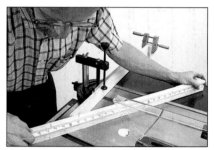

Checking length of rails

material back, check it for accuracy, and, if necessary, reset the length stop. Flip the rail over and make the cut from the opposite side. The nick will never show. This same procedure works well when cutting mullions and muntins, too.

Next, clamp the rails and the stiles together as shown in the photo *below* (note the placement of the clamps). Measure as shown to find the length of the mullion, then cut it
continued

Measuring length of mullion

BASIC CABINET CONSTRUCTION
continued

to length. Now, remove the clamps from the frame, line up the ends of the top and bottom rails, and mark the location of the mullion as shown *below*. Use the same procedure to find the length of the muntins, then cut them to length.

Lay out the face frame parts. If any of the parts happen to be

Marking position of mullion

crowned (you can check this by sighting down the face of each board), the crown must face out (see the sketch *below*). Mark the face of each part, then clamp all of them together. Once you have the parts aligned and in their proper spots, make two marks across each

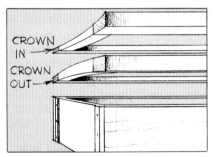

joint line where two members meet (see the photo *below*). Also mark each joint as A-A, B-B, and so on to avoid mixing up the parts.

Marking dowel pin locations

Remove the clamps from the frame and then drill dowel holes, using your marks as a guide. Remember that you want the combined depth of the mating holes ¹⁄₁₆" or so deeper than the length of the dowel pins you're using.

Now, insert glued dowel pins into the holes you've bored, and assemble the frame—from the inside out. Use clamps to hold joints tight. While the glue is still wet, check for square, and rack the frame into square, if necessary. See the sketch *below* for how to do this.

When the glue dries, remove the clamps and sand the face frame smooth.

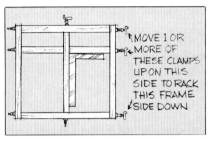

Attach the face frame to the carcass

Glue and clamp the frame to the carcass, making sure that the top of the bottom rail aligns with the top of the carcass bottom, and that the frame overlaps both cabinet ends evenly (see the photo *below*). When everything aligns properly, drive finish nails through the frame and into the carcass sides and bottom.

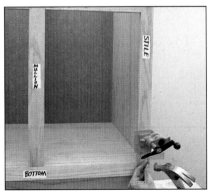

Attaching the face frame

Centering divider behind mullion

Before nailing the mullion to the divider panel, be sure that you center the panel behind the mullion. Clamp the two members together as shown in the photograph *above* and then drive your nails.

Cut and install the shelves

Usually, shelves measure ⅛" narrower than the width of the cavity into which they fit and ⅛" shorter than the distance from the cabinet's back to the back side of the face frame, so you shouldn't have any difficulty figuring their size.

Most cabinetmakers band the front edges of shelves with thin strips of a wood that's compatible with that being used on the cabinet. But you also can band them with wood veneer tape, if you wish. Either way, be sure to figure

Positioning holes for shelf clips

the thickness of the material used into your calculations.

Cut the shelves to size, then test-fit them to make sure there's sufficient play to accommodate the shelf clips you'll be installing later.

The photo *at the bottom of the previous column* shows about the easiest way we know of to position the holes for shelf clips. The perforated hardboard serves as a template that ensures that the holes on either side of the shelves align exactly. Set the template on the cabinet bottom and against one of the end panels and drill a series of holes. Then, with the template in the same relative position, move it to the opposite panel and drill another series of holes using the same guide holes as before.

Note: *If you drill holes into both sides of the divider, you'll need to offset one set from the other.*

Building the door and drawer fronts

With *slab-type* doors and drawers, you simply cut the panels to the appropriate size, band or veneer the edges, and perhaps decorate the panel. But the *frame-and-panel* option consists of a joined frame into which a variety of inserts can go. In our example, we've chosen to go with a frame that fits together with dowels, just as the face frame did. We've also opted for *overlay* doors and drawers rather than the *lipped* or *flush* type.

Typically, doors and drawer fronts overlap their openings by ¼" all around (the hinge configuration can alter this somewhat). In our example, to figure the size frames you need, add ½" to both the height and width of each opening. Then, cut the frame parts to size (rails fit between the stiles here, too).

You machine and assemble these frames somewhat differently than you did the face frames. If you go with thin plywood panel inserts, you may want to cut a groove in the center of the inside edge of the frame members, and insert the panel as you assemble the frame. For glass or other inserts, you

Routing back side of door

assemble the frame first, then rout out a rabbet on the back side of the frame (see the photo *above*) to accept the material. (Since we decorated the fronts of the doors and drawer with a pattern along the inside edges, we used the latter technique.)

Hang the doors

Begin by screwing the hinges to the doors. (A general rule of thumb here calls for the hinges to be "a hinge-length in" from the top and bottom of the doors.) Then, position one of the doors over its opening as shown *below* (door must overlap opening evenly).

Now, mark the position of the hinge mounting holes on the stiles, drill pilot holes, and hang the doors.

Build and install the drawers

Drawers certainly can be made in several different ways, but we've

Positioning door over opening

chosen to make ours with side-mount drawer slides and a drawer front that screws onto the drawer

assembly. (Door fronts that are independent of the drawer allow you to change the look of a cabinet at a later date if you want without totally rebuilding the door.)

First, cut and fasten drawer-mount blocks to one end panel and the divider panel. (The bottom of the block should align with the top of the muntin below the opening.) The idea is to provide a surface on which the drawer slide can bear: you'll want the block thick enough so that its face is flush with the inside edge of the stile and mullion.

How you size the drawers varies depending on the type of slide you use. With side-mount type drawer slides, you'll usually want the width of the drawer to be 1" narrower than the width of the opening (check the drawer slide package instructions to make sure). The height of the drawer parts should be ¼" shorter than the height of the drawer opening. And as for the drawer's depth, most cabinetmakers stop it just short of the depth of the cabinet. For example, if the distance from the front of the face frame to the cabinet back measures 23", you'd want the drawer 22½" at most.

Now, cut the drawer parts to size and assemble them as shown in the photo below. Note that both ends of the drawer sides have rabbets that accept the front and back, and that all four sides of the box have ¼" grooves ½" up from the bottom edge to accept the drawer bottom.

continued

Assembling the drawer

BASIC CABINET CONSTRUCTION
continued

Install the drawer slides according to manufacturer's instructions. Then, put the drawer in the cavity, stick a couple of pieces of two-sided tape to its face, and position the drawer front as shown in the photo *below*. When you're satisfied with the front's position, squeeze the front and the drawer together, pull the drawer

Positioning the drawer front

partway out, and clamp the two together. Remove the drawer from the cavity and screw the drawer front to the drawer as shown here. (You'll undoubtedly have to shim and adjust the drawer slides to square the front with the face frame and to achieve a tight fit, and that can require patience. We use cardboard for our shims.)

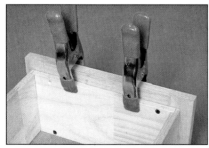

Screwing front to drawer

Attaching a false front

In some cabinetmaking situations, such as in our example, plumbing fixtures or other items make it impractical if not impossible to put a drawer where one would normally be. So what do you do? False fronts to the rescue!

You build false fronts exactly as you do the fronts of drawers. But instead of screwing the front to a drawer, you fasten false fronts to the face frame with cleats. The photo *right* shows you how. Align the front with the other doors and drawers on the cabinet before you tighten the cleats to the back side of the face frame.

Add a cabinet top

You can either purchase a commercially available top for your cabinet or build it yourself. We site-built ours, then covered it with plastic laminate. It's easy!

For tops without backsplashes, cut a piece of ¾" plywood ½" wider and ¼" deeper than the cabinet. Now, face the front and sides of the cabinet with ¾"x1½"-strips on edge. Cover all exposed surfaces with plastic laminate, starting with the side edges, the front, and finally the top. Place the counter on the cabinet, scribe it to the wall if necessary, then fasten the top to the cabinet with metal angles.

If you want to add a backsplash, cut a ¾" plywood countertop that measures ½" wider than the cabinet, and ¼" deeper than the cabinet less the thickness of the backsplash. Band the front and both sides with ¾"x1½" strips on edge.

Attaching false front with cleats

Now, for the backsplash, cut a piece of ¾" plywood the width of the countertop, less the combined thickness of the scribe strip material that fastens to both ends of the backsplash. (The scribe strip allows you to custom-fit the cabinet to the wall.) Fasten the strips to the ¾" plywood as shown *below*.

Next, cover the counter with plastic laminate, starting with the side edges, the front, and the top. Do the same to the backsplash—ends first, the top, and the front.

Now, screw the backsplash to the counter, set the cabinet and countertop in place, scribe the backsplash to fit snugly against the wall (if necessary), and fasten the top to the cabinet with metal angles.

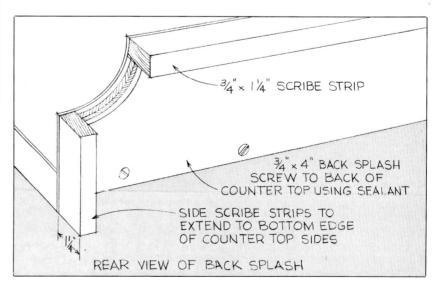

¾" × 1¼" SCRIBE STRIP

¾" × 4" BACK SPLASH
SCREW TO BACK OF
COUNTER TOP USING SEALANT

SIDE SCRIBE STRIPS TO
EXTEND TO BOTTOM EDGE
OF COUNTER TOP SIDES

1½"
4

REAR VIEW OF BACK SPLASH

PICTURE-PERFECT MITER JOINTS

The picture-perfect miter joint—is it possible to accomplish? We think so, and we're sure you'll agree with us after you master the easy-to-learn tricks and techniques we share with you here.

Lots of home hobbyists have a terrible time making accurate miter joints. Many a can of wood putty has been forced into the crevices between two "almost accurately cut" pieces of wood. While that's great for putty manufacturers, it doesn't say much for the level of craftsmanship.

Actually, simple miter joints aren't any more difficult to make than an accurately done butt joint, for example. In fact, you can make any joint well if you follow the Golden Rules of Joint Making.

Rule 1—Use a sharp saw or blade to make the cuts

Rule 2—Set up your saw accurately

Rule 3—Test the setup on scrap before cutting

Rule 4—Learn how to compensate for the minor fitting problems you'll encounter

Note: *We restrict our comments to simple miter joints with splines. (For more information on why we fortify our miter joints with splines, as well as a look at seven different splining options, see pages 40 and 41.)*

Determine the miter angle

Though most people think of a miter joint as two boards meeting at a 90° angle, that needn't always be the case. That's why you must first determine the miter angle you're dealing with.

The sketch at the *top of the next column* shows that no matter what

situation you're in, *the miter angle equals exactly half the joint angle.*

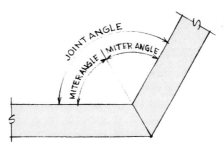

When dealing with two boards that meet at an angle, there are basically three ways to figure the miter angle.

The sketch *below* shows a full-circle protractor (a handy workshop tool if you don't already have one) figuring the miter angle. This tool works well if you're dealing with a

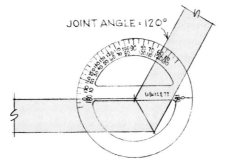

JOINT ANGLE = 120°

flat surface. You simply position the center point of the protractor at the joint line, with the scale at zero on one of the joining members. Read the joint angle as shown. The miter angle in this example is 60°.

On occasion, you'll need a sliding T-bevel to figure the angle (see the sketch in the *next column*). Align the tool's pivot point with the joint and tighten the setscrew to record the angle. Draw the angle on a piece of paper or a flat surface, then measure with your protractor to get an exact reading in

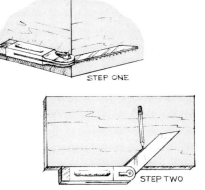

STEP ONE

STEP TWO

STEP THREE

degrees. The miter angle would be half of the reading.

Here's a handy formula that makes figuring the miter angle a snap in situations other than those described above.

The miter angle = 360° ÷ number of sides ÷ 2.

For example, in building a six-sided project, the miter angle would be 360° ÷ 6 ÷ 2 = 30°.

Find the length of each piece

With squares and rectangles, you shouldn't have any trouble doing this. Just measure the lengths needed and begin your saw setup.

The plot thickens a bit when you're dealing with other geometric shapes. Fortunately, though, we've devised an easy way to figure length for these. The top sketch on *page 38* shows how it's done.

Start by scribing a circle (on scratch paper) that defines the outside perimeter of the item you
continued

PICTURE-PERFECT MITER JOINTS
continued

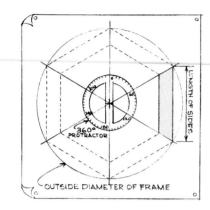

want to make. Then, lay a full-circle protractor on the center point of the circle and make marks to divide the circle into the correct number of segments. Extend lines from the center point through your marks and on out to the perimeter. The distance from one intersection of lines and the perimeter to the next intersection equals the length of each piece.

Set up your saw accurately

Consider yourself fortunate if you can move your saw to, say, 45° and be dead on the money. Most equipment simply isn't that accurate. But, you have to start somewhere, so set your saw at the appropriate angle (the miter box we used in the photo *below* has positive stops at some of the more common angle settings).

Make your test cuts

Doing this will tell you a lot in a hurry. If you're making a square frame, for example, make a cut at one end of a pair of test scraps and then check the accuracy of the angle with a framing or try square

The sketch *below* shows what can occur if the angle isn't right on. If the toes touch, you need to increase the angle of cut. But if the heels come together, decrease the angle slightly.

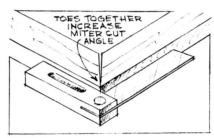

Repeat this process until the joining members meet perfectly. Though time-consuming, you'll find this chore beneficial in the end.

Set up for length

Once you've verified the accuracy of the angle of cut, you can then turn your attention to ensuring the correct length of each member. How you do this varies depending on the type of project you're working on.

With projects such as picture frames and the like, we miter-cut one end of each of the pieces first, set up a length stop (see the photo *below*) and then cut the other end of each piece. Length stops come in handy no matter what tool you're using to make your miter cuts. They sure beat trying to measure each piece separately.

Sometimes, when you're building a large project or dealing with long pieces of material, it's not possible

to set up a length stop. In these situations, we cut one end of a piece, then measure very carefully, mark the cutoff line, and make the second cut. *When marking the cutoff line, be sure to indicate which side of the line you want the blade to be on when you make the second cut.*

Dry-fit and make minor adjustments

By now, you should have a pretty good fit. To be sure, though, clamp the parts together. When we clamped the frame shown in the photo *below*, we detected a minor problem.

We scribed a line on one of the adjacent parts, then used a block plane to remove the excess wood from the heel portion of the miter (see the photo *below*). If you use a block plane, work from the heel edge toward the toe to avoid tear-out.

Disk sanders make quick work of minor irregularities, too (see the

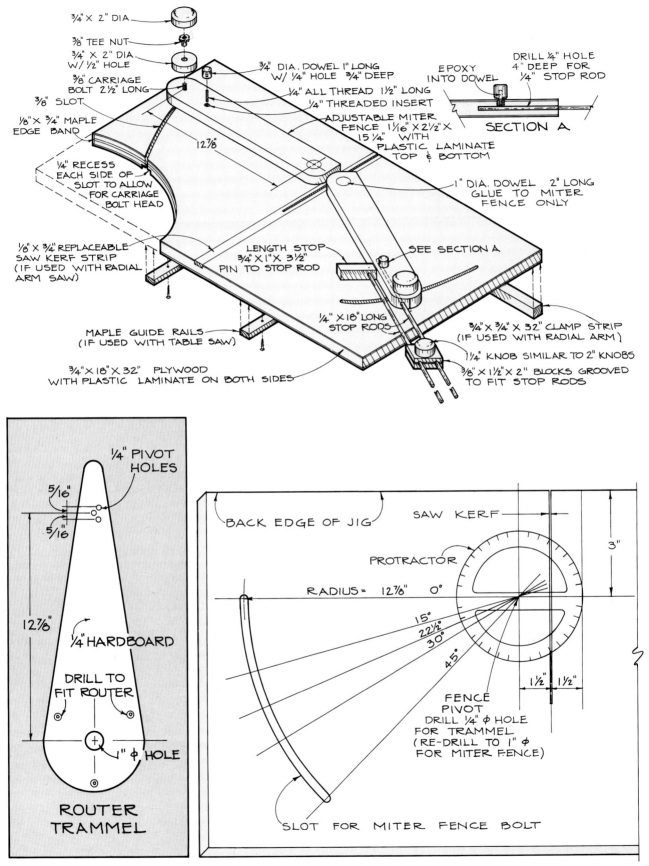

3/4" X 2" DIA.

3/8" TEE NUT

3/4" X 2" DIA.
W/ 1/2" HOLE

3/8" CARRIAGE
BOLT 2 1/2" LONG

3/8" SLOT

1/8" X 3/4" MAPLE
EDGE BAND

3/4" DIA. DOWEL 1" LONG
W/ 1/4" HOLE 3/4" DEEP

1/4" ALL THREAD 1 1/2" LONG
1/4" THREADED INSERT

ADJUSTABLE MITER
FENCE 1 1/16" X 2 1/2" X
15 1/4" WITH
PLASTIC LAMINATE
TOP & BOTTOM

12 7/8"

1/4" RECESS
EACH SIDE OF
SLOT TO ALLOW
FOR CARRIAGE
BOLT HEAD

1/8" X 3/4" REPLACEABLE
SAW KERF STRIP
(IF USED WITH RADIAL
ARM SAW)

LENGTH STOP
3/4" X 1" X 3 1/2"
PIN TO STOP ROD

SEE SECTION A

1" DIA. DOWEL 2" LONG
GLUE TO MITER
FENCE ONLY

EPOXY
INTO DOWEL

DRILL 1/4" HOLE
4" DEEP FOR
1/4" STOP ROD

SECTION A

MAPLE GUIDE RAILS
(IF USED WITH TABLE SAW)

1/4" X 18" LONG
STOP RODS

3/4" X 18" X 32" PLYWOOD
WITH PLASTIC LAMINATE ON BOTH SIDES

3/4" X 3/4" X 32" CLAMP STRIP
(IF USED WITH RADIAL ARM)

1 1/4" KNOB SIMILAR TO 2" KNOBS

3/8" X 1 1/2" X 2" BLOCKS GROOVED
TO FIT STOP RODS

1/4" PIVOT
HOLES

5/16"

5/16"

12 7/8"

1/4" HARDBOARD

DRILL TO
FIT ROUTER

1" φ HOLE

ROUTER
TRAMMEL

BACK EDGE OF JIG

SAW KERF

PROTRACTOR

3"

RADIUS = 12 7/8"   0°

15°
22 1/2°
30°

45°

1 1/2" 1 1/2"

FENCE
PIVOT
DRILL 1/4" φ HOLE
FOR TRAMMEL
(RE-DRILL TO 1" φ
FOR MITER FENCE)

SLOT FOR MITER FENCE BOLT

continued

39

PICTURE-PERFECT MITER JOINTS
continued

photo *above*). If you have one of these tools, you'll probably want to go this route rather than using the much-slower block plane.

A miter-cutting jig for your table or radial arm saw

If you make lots of picture frames or other projects that utilize miter joints, do we have a jig for you! The sketch at the *top of page 39* shows how it goes together. The two adjustable miter fences pivot on 1" walnut dowels. By loosening the 2" walnut knob at the end of each fence, you can rotate the fences to any angle you wish. In one of the other sketches on *page 39*, we show you how to plot several commonly used angles on the jig's top surface for easy reference.

Note also, in the plan drawing of the jig, that we've incorporated a length stop adjustment mechanism to provide for positive length control.

The photo *below* and the accompanying router trammel sketch on *page 39* show how we routed the recesses in the jig's underside (the ⅜" carriage bolt fastened to the 2" knob moves back and forth in the slot). First, we routed the ⅜" slot, then a ¼" recess

on each side of the slot to allow for the head of the carriage bolt.

Note: *When making cuts with this jig, you'll have to remove one or the other of the fences to make way for the stock you're mitering and also to prevent cut-off pieces from wedging between the blade and the fence. The fences simply unscrew and lift off.*

Several ways to reinforce your miter joints

We like to strengthen our miter joints. And one of the best ways we've found to beef them up is with splines. Splines not only strengthen the joint by providing more surface area for the glue to adhere to, they also make it a great deal easier for you to glue and clamp your project. And some types of splines even make the joint more attractive.

For your convenience, we've developed a visual chart showing seven different ways to strengthen your miter joints. In the first photo of each category, we show the finished joint. The three photos that follow show how to make it.

THROUGH SPLINE
For greatest strength, crosscut spline material

Cutting groove with jig

Cutting spline material*
****We use hot-melt glue to adhere blocks to the stock***

Clamping with glue blocks**

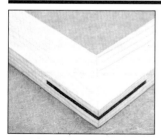

FEATHER SPLINE

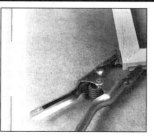

Joint glued and clamped

Cut groove with V-block jig

Spline inserted and clamped

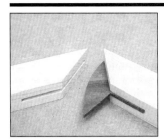

CONCEALED SPLINE

Cutting groove using stop block

Shaping spline to fit groove

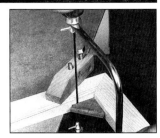

Trimming away excess spline

HIDDEN SPLINE

Cutting mortise with router*   *Note sequence of cuts 1 and 2

Rounding ends of spline

Spline in place; assembling joint

EDGE SPLINE

Cutting miters

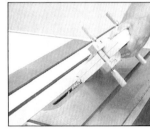

Paired parts being grooved* *Clamping together ensures a perfect fit

Assembling joint with glue

MULTI-FEATHER

Cutting grooves with jig* *See the sketch on page 44 for how to build this jig

Clamping spline material

Sanding excess spline

DOVETAIL KEY

Cutting dovetail with router

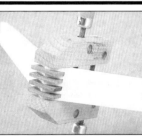

Ripping spline material* *Cut spline material at same angle as that cut by the router bit

Gluing and inserting spline keys

continued

PICTURE-PERFECT MITER JOINTS
continued

Gluing and clamping procedures

It's hard to overemphasize the importance of correct gluing and clamping technique. Without it, miter joints never look "quite right." Luckily, though, there's nothing involved that you can't learn quickly.

Selecting and applying glue

Before doing any gluing and clamping, of course, you need to select the right glue for the task at hand. On most projects, we rely on the yellow woodworker's glue. But, if the project requires a glue with a bit more working time, we go with one of the polyvinyl acetate (white) glues. What about those situations that require a waterproof glue? We reach for the resorcinol or waterproof epoxy, the only truly waterproof glues. We like epoxy glue because of the strong bond it creates.

When we need a glue that sets up incredibly quickly, we haul out our hot-melt glue gun for simple jobs, or the hot-melt hide glue pot for the larger projects.

Photo A depicts how we apply yellow or white glue. We cover both joining surfaces with a thin layer of glue (a pencil brush makes an ideal applicator). We've found that the pencil brush deposits a sufficient amount of glue to do the job, but it doesn't give us a great deal of squeeze-out to remove. Note also that we keep a cup of water nearby to keep the brush wet between uses. (Be sure to wipe the bristles dry before using it to apply more glue.)

Hot-melt gun glues, though not one of the strongest types available, do come in handy in many situations. In photo B, you'll notice that only hand pressure is necessary, and then only for 20 to 30 seconds.

When using hot-melt glue, keep in mind that it is HOT as it comes from the gun or pot, so be careful

A

B

not to get burned. Also remember that you must work quickly or the glue will set up before you're ready. We've found that you have to slide the mating parts back and forth over each other to squeeze as much glue out as possible before it sets. Otherwise, it actually keeps the joint from closing properly.

Clamping four-sided frames

In photos C and D on the *next page*, we show two ways to clamp four-sided frames. In the first, we use four miter clamps. These work well, but a less-expensive option is to make your own clamping system. The sketch on the *top of the next page* shows how.

C

D

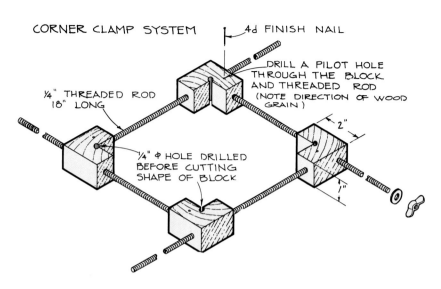

CORNER CLAMP SYSTEM

4d FINISH NAIL

DRILL A PILOT HOLE
THROUGH THE BLOCK
AND THREADED ROD
(NOTE DIRECTION OF WOOD
GRAIN)

¼" THREADED ROD
18" LONG

¼" Ø HOLE DRILLED
BEFORE CUTTING
SHAPE OF BLOCK

2"

1"

Clamping boxes

When gluing up cabinet carcasses and the like, you always need plenty of bar or pipe clamps. You'll also find our pipe clamp pads handy when it comes time to put the squeeze on your project. The pads allow you to apply uniform pressure along the length of the carcass.

Photo E *right* shows the pads in use and the accompanying sketch *below right* shows how to construct this simple-to-make device. After you're through with them, drill a hole in the end of each and hang them somewhere nearby.

Clamping items with more than four sides

Some hobbyists panic when it comes to clamping many-sided or odd-shaped projects. And granted, applying pressure in these situations can be difficult. But we've found that web clamps can come to your rescue in those difficult-to-deal-with scenarios.

In photos F and G at the *top of page 44,* we show how to clamp an octagonal frame and a larger hexagonal project. Note that the half-round clamp pads help keep the straps from damaging the veneer edges.

continued

E

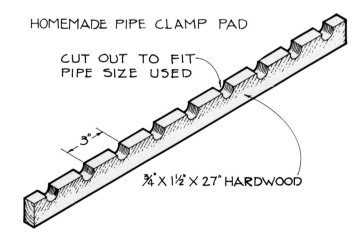

HOMEMADE PIPE CLAMP PAD

CUT OUT TO FIT
PIPE SIZE USED

3"

¾" X 1½" X 27" HARDWOOD

PICTURE-PERFECT MITER JOINTS
continued

How to use the multi-feather joint jig

1. Adjust the saw blade to proper height (approximately 1" above saw table for ¾" stock).

2. Place the jig on saw table and pass it across stopped saw blade to check alignment.

3. Place stock against spacing guide and make first cut. Test with scrap first.

4. Lift the stock and reposition, with the first cut over the spacing guide.

5. Repeat step 4 for additional cuts.

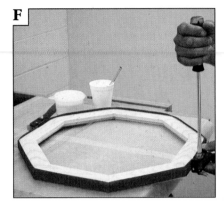

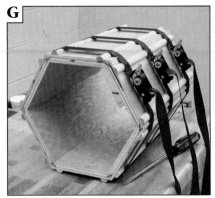

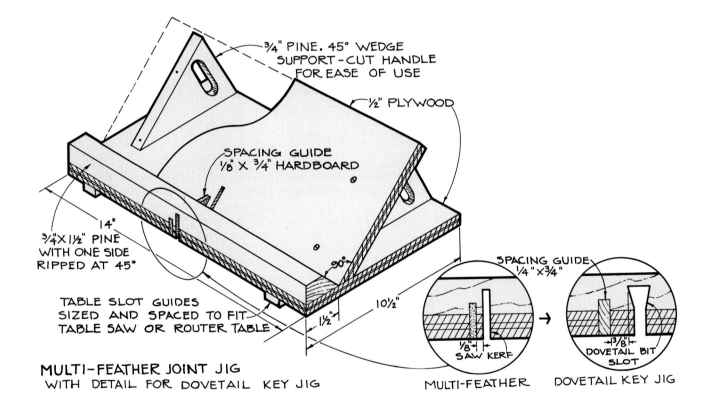

¾" PINE. 45° WEDGE SUPPORT-CUT HANDLE FOR EASE OF USE

½" PLYWOOD

SPACING GUIDE ⅛" X ¾" HARDBOARD

14"

¾" X 1½" PINE WITH ONE SIDE RIPPED AT 45°

90°

10½"

1½"

TABLE SLOT GUIDES SIZED AND SPACED TO FIT TABLE SAW OR ROUTER TABLE

SPACING GUIDE ¼" X ¾"

⅛" SAW KERF

⅜" DOVETAIL BIT SLOT

MULTI-FEATHER JOINT JIG
WITH DETAIL FOR DOVETAIL KEY JIG

MULTI-FEATHER

DOVETAIL KEY JIG

BASIC RAISED PANEL CONSTRUCTION

Building beautiful raised panels has never been easier. With today's generation of tools, cutters, and some easy-to-master techniques, you can become a panel-raising pro in no time at all. Come on, give it a try; you'll be glad you did!

Raised panel construction looks much more difficult than it actually is. As you can see in the anatomy sketch below, raised panels have only three components: rails, stiles, and a panel. You can fashion all three using any furniture-quality wood you want—softwood or hardwood. We use ¾" thick material for the stiles and rails, and ½" solid stock for the panels.

Both the stills and rails have grooves along their inside edge to accept the panel, which has a chamfered border along each of its edges. Typically, the grooves measure ¼" wide and deep.

How to figure rail and stile size

The width and length of the rails and stiles depend on two factors: the overall scale of the project and the dimensions of, say, the door opening, if you're building a cabinet door, or the size of the panel if you're using it as a furniture or cabinet carcass component (sides, back, etc.). In the example we've chosen, both the rails and stiles measure 1½" wide. But on larger-scale panels, you'll often see stiles that are as wide as 2" and rails as wide as 3"

Figuring the length of stiles is easy; you just measure the length needed to cover or fill the opening and cut them to length. But with the rails, determining length may call for some math. Here's the formula that applies to the two types of joinery we cover in this article—*tenon spline butt joints* and *molded and coped joints:*

1) Measure total width of frame.

2) Subtract total width of both stiles. The remainder is the length of the rail. (If you are using molded and coped joinery, proceed to step 3.)

3) Add the combined depth of both stile grooves.

Determine the panel size

Once you know the dimensions of the frame, you can then easily figure the finished size of the panel, too. Just measure the inside distance from stile to stile and rail to rail, add the combined depths of the grooves to the width and height of the panel, then subtract ¹⁄₁₆" from both the width and height. There you have it, almost!

How to figure the panel raise and chamfer exposure

The last things you have to decide are how high to raise the panel and how much chamfer exposure you want. Here again, scale comes into play. Obviously, small-scale panels require a narrower exposure than larger projects. In our example, the exposure measures 1¼" all around, and the *shoulder* (the distance between the face of the panel and the chamfer) is ⅛"-both typical measurements.

The sketch *below* shows how to make sure that the panel will fit snugly in the frame grooves after you make the chamfer cuts. As you can see, the idea is to ensure that at the point of contact between the frame and the panel the thickness of the panel equals the width of the groove. No matter what panel-raising situation you find yourself in, just follow the 5-step marking sequence shown in the sketch.

Why raised panels must float

We said earlier that when figuring the final size of the panel,

continued

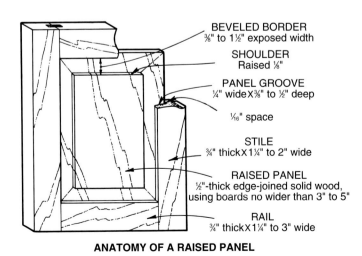

BEVELED BORDER
⅜" to 1½" exposed width

SHOULDER
Raised ⅛"

PANEL GROOVE
¼" wide X ⅜" to ½" deep

¹⁄₁₆" space

STILE
¾" thick X 1¼" to 2" wide

RAISED PANEL
½"-thick edge-joined solid wood, using boards no wider than 3" to 5"

RAIL
¾" thick X 1¼" to 3" wide

ANATOMY OF A RAISED PANEL

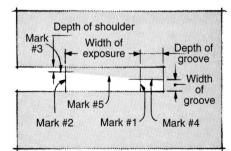

Depth of shoulder

Mark #3

Width of exposure

Depth of groove

Width of groove

Mark #5

Mark #2   Mark #1   Mark #4

BASIC RAISED PANEL CONSTRUCTION
continued

you need to measure the distance between the inside edges of the stiles and between the rails, add the combined depth of the grooves, and subtract ¹⁄₁₆" from the final length and width of the panel. But we didn't say why. The reason: Wood shrinks and expands as it dries or absorbs humidity from the air. Since there is nothing any of us can do to stop it, we must allow for it. The ¹⁄₁₆" space allows the panel to expand without forcing the rail/stile joint apart. That's also why knowledgeable woodworkers never glue the panel into the frame grooves.

Two basic style options to choose from

When building raised panels, you have quite a few options to choose from in terms of how you want to join the stiles to the rails, including various types of mortise-and-tenon joints. But basically, you have only two style options: *squared-edge frames and molded-edge frames,* both of which we show *below.*

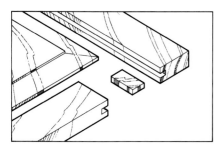

Square-edged frame

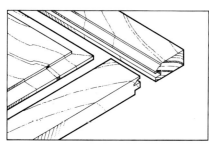

Molded and coped frame

What we've decided to do here is show you one good, easy way to make each type.

Conceivably, after you've had some experience building raised panels, you may want to try a few modifications. But either of the systems we show here will enable you to produce beautifully crafted raised panels that you'll be proud to show off.

We build the squared-edge type entirely with a table saw or a radial-arm saw. The molded-edge type, though, can be accomplished with a combination of table saw and router table, or with the router table alone.

How to make a squared-edge framed panel using tenon spline joinery

Make no mistake about it! Just because what you're about to learn is easy doesn't mean that the framed panel you build is in any way inferior. It's not! In fact, we make most of our framed panels using the steps that follow. (You can use a table saw or a radial arm saw to make all the cuts.)

Preparing the rails and stiles

Start by ripping and crosscutting the stiles and rails to size. (You may want to refer to the section "How to Figure Rail and Stile Size.") Then, lay out the pieces as they will be when you finish the panel, and mark the face of each piece as well as each joint line. After doing this, you can then cut a groove along the inside edge of each member. (Remember: always run the face side against the rip fence so the groove will be in the same position on each frame member.) Now, using the same saw setup, cut grooves along the ends of both rails as shown in photograph A at the *top of the next column.* Notice that we used a follow block to help push the rails through the saw.

A follow block adds stability and prevents chipout of the workpiece.

Using scrap material (we use the same wood as that used for the frame pieces), cut the spline material to size. The splines need to be as thick as the grooves are wide and as wide as the combined depth of the grooves less ¹⁄₁₆" to allow for expansion.

Now, dry-clamp the frame members and splines to check for a good fit and so that you can measure the opening the panel will fit into. When measuring, make sure not to forget to figure in the depth of the grooves.

Note: *To give you the best possible view in our photos, we did not always use safety guards. However, we STRONGLY RECOMMEND that you use safety devices whenever possible in your shop.*

Making up the panel

With measurements in hand, you can then make up the panel. (We use ½" stock for most of our panels because it allows us to raise the panel and yet not have the face of the panel protrude beyond the face of the frame. We also make up our panels from boards that measure no greater than 4" wide. Doing so allows us to plane or resaw the board thickness down to ½". You also can purchase ½" stock at many lumber outlets and by mail order.) Once you have made up the panel, remove glue squeeze-out and cut the panel according to your measurements.

Raising the panel

Now comes the fun part! Start by laying out the cut marks on one of the panel's edges as described in the section titled "How to Figure the Panel Raise and Chamfer Exposure." Then, set up your saw and make the *shoulder cuts* on the face of the panel as shown in photograph B *below*. (You'll want the saw cut to equal the depth of the shoulder.)

Since it's almost impossible to measure a saw blade's bevel to within 1 degree, we crank the blade to an angle and height that looks about right, then we eyeball both as shown in photograph C

Determining the position of the rip fence.

The panel-raising sequence begins when you make shoulder cuts along the edges of the glued-up panel.

Eyeball the angle and height of cut, then, using scrap, fine-tune your guess.

A wide auxiliary fence helps stabilize the panel.

left. When we get close, we run some scrap material through the saw, then fine-tune both the angle and height until we're right on the money.

Next, set your rip fence the correct distance from the blade (see photograph D *above*) and make the chamfer cuts. Notice that we have a zero-clearance insert in place for these cuts; it eliminates the possibility of the panel getting hung up on its way through the

blade. Notice also that when running the panel through the saw, we depend on a tall auxiliary fence to steady the panel against (see photograph E *above*). Photograph F at the *top of page 48* shows the chamfer cuts being made with a radial arm saw and an 8" carbide blade fitted with a 4" dampening collar.

After making all the chamfer cuts, dry-clamp the frame/panel

continued

BASIC RAISED PANEL CONSTRUCTION
continued

Alternate method of cutting the chamfered portion of the panel with a radial arm saw.

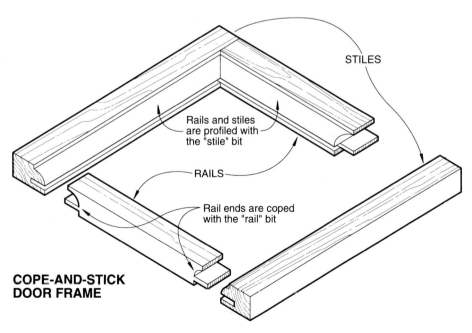

STILES

Rails and stiles are profiled with the "stile" bit

RAILS

Rail ends are coped with the "rail" bit

COPE-AND-STICK DOOR FRAME

assembly to check for a good fit. Then, cut ¹⁄₁₆" from the width and length of the panel to allow it to move freely in the frame grooves. Since the panel will rest in the bottom groove, we cut ¹⁄₁₆" off the top. This ensures a balanced look when the panel is installed.

And finally, sand and otherwise clean up the panel and the inside edge of the frame members. When you're sanding, do so carefully so you don't round over the edges where the pieces join.

How to make cope-and-stick framed panels

If you want framed panels that look like those many commercial woodworking shops make with their shapers, something with a bit more "gingerbread," you'll like the results you'll get with cope-and-stick framed panels. To clear up any confusion you may have over the words "cope" and "stick," the stick or molded area of the stiles and rails is the decorative edging along the inside edge of the frame. You can mold the outer edge, too, if you want. Coping refers to the cutaway portion at each end of both rails that allows the rails to fit snugly against the stiles.

Note: *We used a router table for the following operations to ensure accurate cuts.*

How to master stile-and-rail sets

With a set of these bits, you can make professional-quality cope-and-stick door frames such as the one shown *left*. However, you need to know what to look for when buying a stile-and-rail router bit set, and how to make it work effectively.

We've tried several versions of these sets, and we prefer those with rugged ½" shanks. And, we've had our best luck with the sets that have a bearing between the profile cutter and the slotting cutter on the rail bit as shown in the set in photograph G *below*.

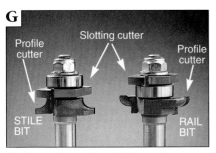

G

Profile cutter
Slotting cutter
Profile cutter
STILE BIT
RAIL BIT

Quality stile-and-rail bit sets have rail bits with pilot bearings between the slotting and profile cutters.

Sets such as these have thin shims between the cutters that may need to be adjusted, so we suggest you make your first cuts in scrap stock. When adjusted, the bits will produce rails and stiles that fit snugly together, with flush faces and profiles that align.

To make a door frame, start by adjusting the stile bit to the height that yields the desired profile. Although called a "stile" bit, this bit cuts the visible profile on both the stiles *and* rails. The "rail" bit makes the coping cut on the ends of the rails.

Adjust the fence so the stile bit's pilot bearing is flush with the fence or barely protrudes from the fence. With the face side down, rout the profile along the inside edge of both stiles as shown in photograph H *top right*.

To cut the coped rail ends, insert the rail bit and adjust its height by holding a profiled stile edge up to it as shown in photograph I *right*. Again, adjust the fence so that the bit's bearing is flush with the fence or just barely protrudes from the fence. With the rails face side down and clamped to a pushblock, make the coped cuts.

Finally, reinsert the stile bit, and profile the inside edges of the rails to match the profiled edge of the stiles. By saving this step for last rather than profiling the stiles and rails at the same time, you can clean up any splintering on the rails caused by the coping cuts.

H

To produce a cope-and-stick door frame, first profile the inside edge of the stiles. If necessary, use feather boards.

I

RAIL BIT

Bottom of the rail bit's slotting cutter and edge of stile should align here

STILE

Adjust the height of the rail cutter by aligning its slotting cutter with one of your stiles.

Making up and raising the panel

After dry-clamping the frame and measuring the dimensions of the panel needed, you make up the panel as described in the earlier section titled "Making up the panel." Then, secure the panel-raising bit in your router, adjust it to the correct height, and raise all four sides of the panel. (It is good practice to rout along the top and bottom of the panel first (across the end grain). Then, when you rout along the panel's sides (with the grain), any previous router tear-out is eliminated.) Dry-clamp the frame and panel together, then trim 1⁄16" from the height and width of the panel. Clean up the frame and panel, and you're ready for final assembly.

continued

BASIC RAISED PANEL CONSTRUCTION
continued

Whatever you do, don't allow glue into the frame's grooves.

Final assembly of the frame and panel

Before actually assembling the framed panel, you should stain and seal the panel itself. If you don't do this, you may notice an unsightly bare mark where the panel and frame meet if the panel ever shifts in the frame (and it will).

We mentioned earlier that the panel must float. That means it's very important that when gluing the frame members together you make sure no glue seeps into the grooves. Photograph J *above* shows the surfaces to which you want to apply glue to the rails. Apply glue to the same area of the stiles, too.

Note: *You may want to drop a few beads of clear silicone sealant into the rail and stile grooves before assembling the panel to prevent rattling.*

Glue and clamp the frame and panel, then lay the unit across a couple of sawhorses and check for square and to see if the panel has accidentally twisted (see photograph K, *top right*). If you can see any daylight under either end of the square, shim the panel as needed and clamp it to the sawhorses.

After the glue has dried, do any final cleanup. (We have found that often it's necessary to use a cabinet scraper—pushed diagonally across the joint lines; see photograph L at *right*—to even out minor height differences.) Then, apply the finish of your choice.

If panel twists during assembly, shim it into adjustment.

To even the surface at the joint lines, scrape diagonally with a cabinet scraper.

MAKING AND INSTALLING DOVETAILED DRAWERS

If you're searching for a straightforward way to make and install sturdy, smooth-sliding drawers that look great, stay tuned. We'll show you how to build dovetailed drawers steered by a simple and inexpensive wooden guide system.

As we sat down to plan this article, we carefully considered the nearly endless options for building a drawer. Eventually, we decided on strong, traditional, ½" half-blind dovetails for joining the sides of the drawer to the front. Any number of commercially available jigs help you make these joints with your router, and we'll share some tips for using them.

To make carcase construction and drawer installation as straightforward as possible, we chose to rest the drawers on ¾" plywood panels. The panels simplify guide installation and make great dust barriers between the drawers.

Let's take an inside look at a basic drawer system

The traditional dovetailed drawer and its cabinet support system must truly be made for each other for effortless operation and a long life. Note, for instance, the key components shown at *right*.

The *drawer* has two ½" *sides* joined to the ½" or ¾" *front* with half-blind dovetails (so named because you can't see the joint from the front of the drawer). Rabbet-and-dado joints hold a ½" *back* to the sides, and a ¼" plywood drawer *bottom* slips into a groove cut into both sides and the front. Note that the sides extend beyond the back to prevent the drawer from dropping to the floor when fully opened.

Fastened to the underside of the drawer bottom are two ¼" *slides* that contact both sides of a ¼" *guide* attached to a ¾" panel beneath each drawer. Together, these parts make up a guide system that channels the drawer straight in and out when pushed and pulled. The guide also serves as a stop that prevents the drawer from striking the back of the carcase when you close the drawer. A *kicker* prevents the drawer from tipping down as you pull it open. You may not need a kicker if the drawer has a ¾" panel just above it.

continued

MAKING AND INSTALLING DOVETAILED DRAWERS
continued

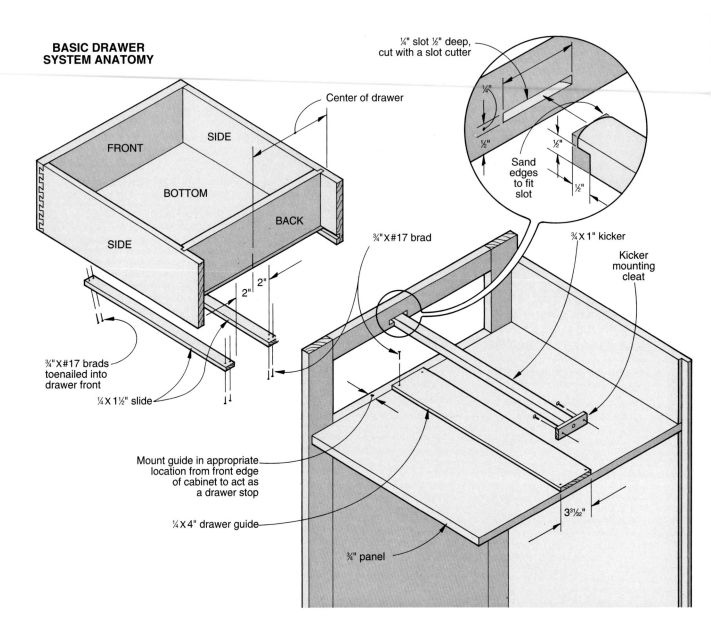

BASIC DRAWER SYSTEM ANATOMY

¼" slot ½" deep, cut with a slot cutter

Center of drawer

SIDE

FRONT

BOTTOM

BACK

SIDE

¼"

½"

½"

½"

Sand edges to fit slot

¾" X #17 brad

¾ X 1" kicker

Kicker mounting cleat

¾" X #17 brads toenailed into drawer front

2" 2"

2"

¼ X 1½" slide

Mount guide in appropriate location from front edge of cabinet to act as a drawer stop

¼ X 4" drawer guide

3³¹⁄₃₂"

¾" panel

Note: *Use a moderately priced, close-grained hardwood such as beech, birch, soft maple or poplar for the drawer sides, back, slides, guides, and kicker; hardwood plywood for the bottom; and drawer fronts that match the cabinet.*

How to size your drawers

Note: *With this type of drawer construction, you need to determine the drawer height when you're planning the cabinet.*

Before you cut the parts for your drawer, you need to decide which of three drawer-front styles to use for your project—flush, lipped, or overlap. Though your decision is mainly one of aesthetics, each style functions slightly differently and also affects the dimensions of some parts. The drawings *on page 53* show and tell how to determine the dimensions of the various drawer parts.

Here we'll construct a drawer with a *flush* front that does not protrude from its surrounding carcase. These fronts make for easy drawer construction, but do require you to carefully fit them and accurately position the drawer guide.

On the other hand, *overlay* and

lipped fronts overlap adjacent edges of the face frame, so you can position the drawers to cover the face frame partially or completely. With these, the overlapping edge acts as a drawer stop.

Since you make a lipped front from a single piece of wood, you must put extra time into cutting the rabbets and setting up your dovetail jig. These extra steps aren't necessary with an overlay front because with this style you simply screw the front (sometimes called a false front) onto the dovetailed drawer front.

Tips on machining the drawer parts

After cutting the drawer parts to size, use a router and a ½" dovetail jig to cut the half-blind dovetails. Most of these jigs work about the same, and all of the models we've tried have adequate instructions for basic use. Here are a few tips that will help ensure success:

• For your comfort, work with the dovetail jig at elbow height. Most workbenches don't reach this high, so you may want to build a simple stand like the one shown *on page 54,* using ¾" stock.

•To prevent mix-ups, number the mating edges of the drawer fronts and sides.

•Take your time in adjusting the jig and setting the depth of the router bit. Your patience will result in tight-fitting joints.

• If you properly cut your dovetailed parts, you need only tap them together gently with a rubber mallet. If they fit with any play, they won't hold up in the long run. If they're too tight, you could break them when forcing them together.

•To reduce the chances of grain tearout, make a skimming cut across the inside face of the drawer side (vertical workpiece) by running the router from right to left across the template as shown *on page 54, bottom left.* Then, cut the dovetails to their full depth by moving the router from left to right, following the notches in the template. Check to make sure you've cut the dovetails completely.

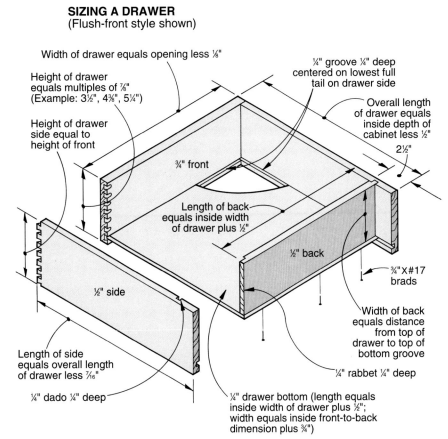

SIZING A DRAWER
(Flush-front style shown)

Width of drawer equals opening less ⅛"

Height of drawer equals multiples of ⅞" (Example: 3½", 4⅜", 5¼")

Height of drawer side equal to height of front

¼" groove ¼" deep centered on lowest full tail on drawer side

Overall length of drawer equals inside depth of cabinet less ½"

2½"

¾" front

Length of back equals inside width of drawer plus ½"

½" back

¾" X #17 brads

Width of back equals distance from top of drawer to top of bottom groove

½" side

Length of side equals overall length of drawer less ⁷⁄₁₆"

¼" dado ¼" deep

¼" rabbet ¼" deep

¼" drawer bottom (length equals inside width of drawer plus ½"; width equals inside front-to-back dimension plus ¾")

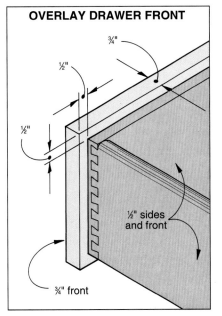

OVERLAY DRAWER FRONT

¾"

½"

½"

½" sides and front

¾" front

LIPPED DRAWER FRONT

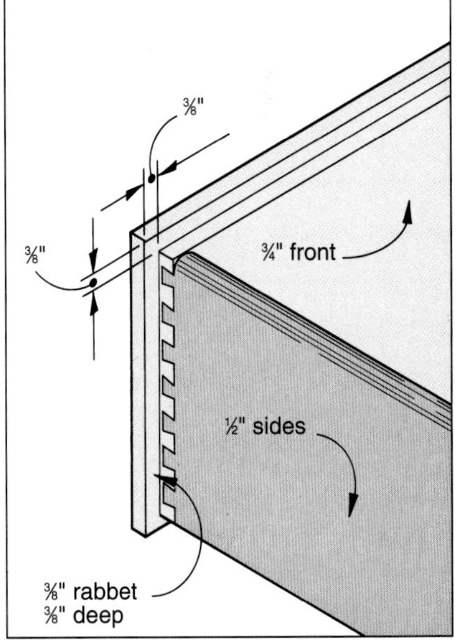

⅜"

⅜"

¾" front

½" sides

⅜" rabbet ⅜" deep

After cutting the dovetails, round over the top edges of the sides and back with a ¼" roundover bit. Then, turning to your tablesaw and dado blade adjusted for a ¼"-wide kerf, cut a ¼ x ¼" groove (to hold the

bottom) into the front and sides. Without changing the height of your dado blade, cut a dado (for the back) into the sides as shown in the photo *on page 54, bottom right.*

continued

MAKING AND INSTALLING DOVETAILED DRAWERS
continued

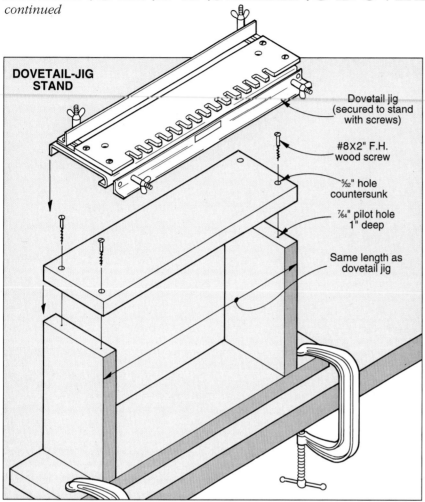

DOVETAIL-JIG STAND

Dovetail jig (secured to stand with screws)

#8X2" F.H. wood screw

⁵⁄₃₂" hole countersunk

⁷⁄₆₄" pilot hole 1" deep

Same length as dovetail jig

Safety note: *Since we're not cutting completely through the workpiece in the photo* below right *we can safely butt the workpiece against the fence. Do not attempt this when cutting all the way through narrow pieces.*

Now, slide the tablesaw fence up to the dado blade and cut the rabbets on the ends of the back. To prevent damage to your fence, clamp or screw a wooden auxiliary fence to it.

Let's assemble the drawer

Before applying glue to the parts, dry clamp the drawer together to check for fit and squareness. Then, apply woodworker's glue to both surfaces of the dovetail joints (a ½"-wide brush works well), and to the rabbet-and-dado joints. Attach one side to the front and back, and then attach the other side. Clamp this assembly together as shown *on page 55, bottom left*. Check the drawer for square by measuring across both diagonally opposing corners. If one diagonal measures longer than the other, adjust your clamps until the diagonal measurements equal one another. Make certain that the drawer back does not block the groove that holds the drawer bottom.

After the glue dries, slide the bottom into place and secure it to

Before cutting the dovetails, make a skimming cut to help prevent grain tearout. Make light cuts, but hold the router firmly to maintain control.

Use your tablesaw's fence as a stop when cutting dadoes into the drawer sides for holding the drawer back.

the back with three ¾" brads. Turn the drawer bottom side up and place some weight (such as two one-gallon containers of fluid) onto the center of the bottom. Apply three 1"-long beads of hotmelt glue to the joints between the bottom and sides and bottom and front as shown *below right*. Leave the weight in place until the glue hardens. This prevents the bottom from rattling, and eliminates gaps between the bottom and sides on the inside of the drawer.

How to install the drawer

Since few of us can build a perfectly square, exactly sized drawer, or a perfect opening to place it into, you'll need to make some slight adjustments for a nice fit. First, place the drawer into its opening, and then follow the three-step process *right* for creating uniform clearance all around the drawer.

With the back removed from your project's carcase, install the drawer guide system according to the drawing *on page 56* titled Installing the Drawer Guide System. In Step 1, take care to butt the slides tightly against the guide before nailing them into position. By sawing or jointing ¹⁄₃₂" off the

continued

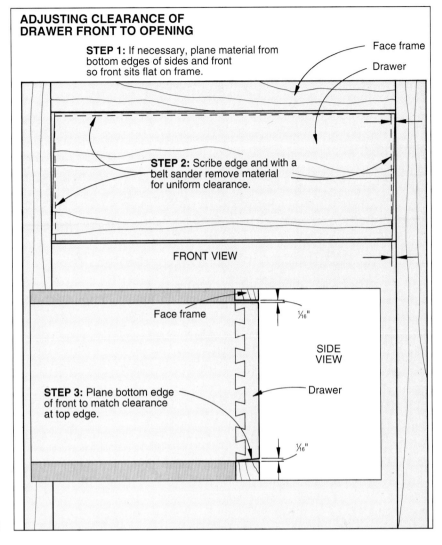

ADJUSTING CLEARANCE OF DRAWER FRONT TO OPENING

STEP 1: If necessary, plane material from bottom edges of sides and front so front sits flat on frame.

Face frame

Drawer

STEP 2: Scribe edge and with a belt sander remove material for uniform clearance.

FRONT VIEW

Face frame

¹⁄₁₆"

SIDE VIEW

Drawer

STEP 3: Plane bottom edge of front to match clearance at top edge.

¹⁄₁₆"

Reposition your clamps slightly to make the drawer square.

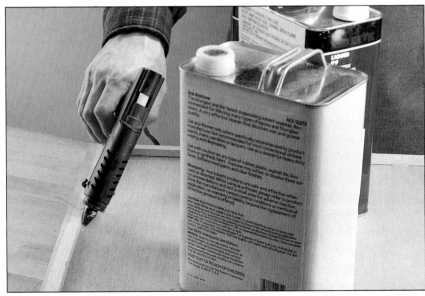

A few beads of hotmelt glue will hold the bottom in place and prevent it from rattling around in its groove.

MAKING AND INSTALLING DOVETAILED DRAWERS
continued

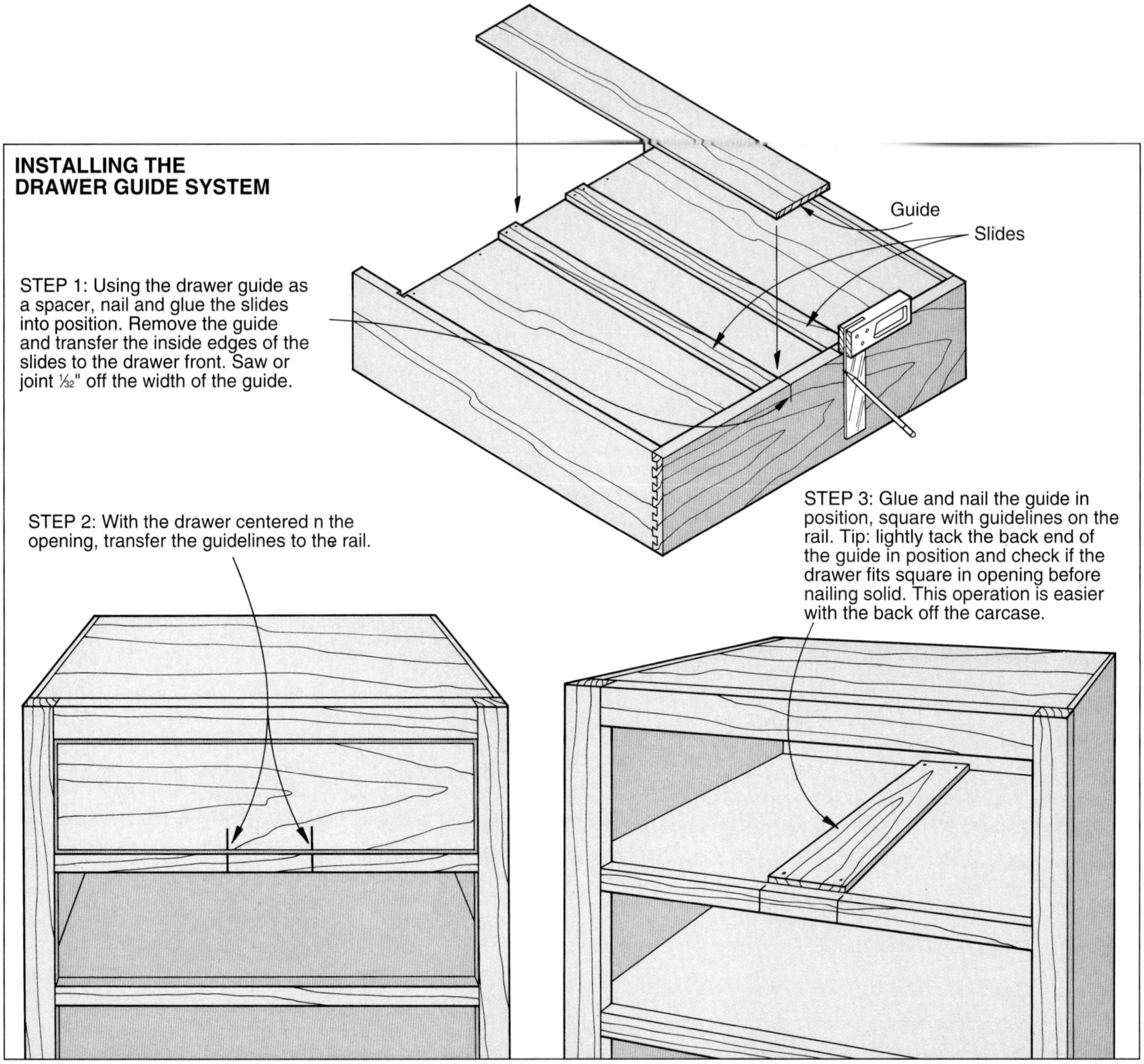

INSTALLING THE DRAWER GUIDE SYSTEM

Guide

Slides

STEP 1: Using the drawer guide as a spacer, nail and glue the slides into position. Remove the guide and transfer the inside edges of the slides to the drawer front. Saw or joint ½" off the width of the guide.

STEP 2: With the drawer centered n the opening, transfer the guidelines to the rail.

STEP 3: Glue and nail the guide in position, square with guidelines on the rail. Tip: lightly tack the back end of the guide in position and check if the drawer fits square in opening before nailing solid. This operation is easier with the back off the carcase.

width of the guide before installing it, you allow the drawer to slide over the guide without excessive play. If the drawer does not have a panel directly above it, then position and secure a kicker according to the drawing and notes on *page 52*.

The final touches

Before applying finish to the drawer, drill any holes necessary for attaching the pull. Then, apply equal amounts of finish to all surfaces of the drawer. This will help prevent the drawer parts from shrinking or expanding at different rates, which could throw the

drawer out of square. Finally, rub paraffin wax onto the bottom surface of the kicker, the bottom edges of the drawer sides, the inside edges of the slides, and the outside edges of the guide for smooth operation.

TEN WINNING WAYS TO WORK WITH PLYWOOD

For all of its virtues—stability, strength, and good looks, to name a few—a sheet of hardwood plywood can present some real challenges to the woodworker. For example, cutting a 4x8' sheet down to size without a lot of rigmarole, or cutting through its thin surface veneer without splintering, can be time-consuming or downright frustrating. And, how do you go about hiding those unsightly edges?

To help you deal with these and other problems peculiar to plywood, we've assembled 10 of our best tips and jigs.

Now, bring on the plywood!

1. How to show your good side when cutting

Circular saw-blade teeth create few splinters as they enter a veneered surface, but may create a lot of chipout as they exit the workpiece. So, always position your stock as shown right.

2. Zero-clearance inserts add up to impressive tablesaw results

To minimize splinters on the underside of the workpiece—something that's especially important with a dado blade—make a zero-clearance insert for your tablesaw. Here's how:

Trace the shape of your tablesaw insert onto a piece of ½" plywood (some smaller saws may require ¼" plywood or tempered hardboard). Cut just along the outside of this line, and then sand back to the line.

To cut the zero-clearance slot in the insert, you first have to install a blade that's at least 1" smaller than the largest blade that the saw handles (9" blade in a 10" saw). The outside blades of a stackable dado set work well if you're

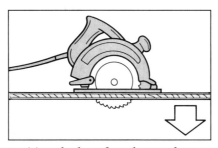

Position the best face down when cutting with a portable circular saw.

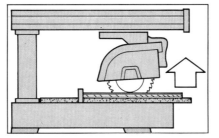

When using a radial-arm saw, position the plywood's best face up.

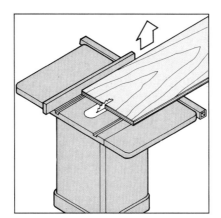

Position the best face up when cutting plywood with a tablesaw.

making the insert for a ⅛"-kerf blade. This is necessary because fully sized blades will interfere with the following steps. If you're making the insert for a dado blade, install the dado blade adjusted to its desired cutting width.

With the saw blade fully lowered, check the fit of the

plywood insert. To set the top of the insert flush with the tablesaw top, apply dabs of hotmelt adhesive to each of the insert supports as shown *below*. Allow these dabs to harden slightly (5–10 seconds should do it), then install the insert and push it down flush with a straightedge as shown below. If the insert sinks too low, just pop it off, apply more hotmelt adhesive, and try again.

Now, cover a portion of the insert with your rip fence. *Be* *continued*

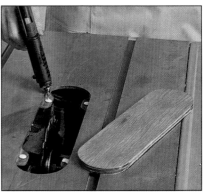

For best results, allow the hotmelt adhesive to cool for 10–15 seconds before putting the insert in place.

Before the hotmelt adhesive cools completely, set the insert flush with the tabletop using a straightedge.

WAYS TO WORK WITH PLYWOOD
continued

Hold down the insert with your rip fence and slowly raise the blade. *Be careful not to cut into the rip fence.*

A straightedge clamped to the bottom side of your workpiece helps you crosscut long panels quickly, easily, and accurately.

careful not to place the rip fence directly above the saw blade. Slowly raise the blade through the insert as shown below. With the blade slot cut, remove the insert and replace the smaller blade with a larger one if necessary.

In the *WOOD®* magazine shop, we make several insert blanks at once so we have one handy whenever we change blades.

3. A hassle-free way to cut long-stock on your tablesaw

Crosscutting a long piece of plywood on a tablesaw can be a dangerous—if not impossible—proposition. It doesn't have to be.

Clamp a straightedge onto the bottom of your workpiece and guide the straightedge along the edge of the tablesaw extension as shown *above right*. If the extension casting has a rough edge, or protruding bolts, you'll have to add a wooden strip to it for the straightedge to glide against. If you add such a strip, make it the necessary thickness so the blade-to-straight-edge distance is a round number.

4. Two ways to gain the upper hand on glue squeeze-out

Glue squeeze-out can do a real number on your finish if allowed to seal the surface of the wood.

Unfortunately, these blemishes usually only reveal themselves after you apply a finish. We use two substances—oil and masking tape—to block squeeze-out from coming in contact with the wood.

As shown *below*, you should first apply the masking tape to surfaces adjoining the dado. Then, dry-fit the mating piece into the dado, and apply tape to the exposed surfaces of this piece. Separate the two pieces, apply glue, clamp, and allow the squeeze-out to form a tough skin before gently peeling away the tape.

Masking tape may not stick to all woods, so we occasionally use Watco natural oil as shown at *right*. First, dry-fit the adjoining pieces, wipe oil where the squeeze-out will occur, separate the pieces, and glue them together. With a sharp chisel, carefully shave away the glue squeeze-out after a tough skin forms.

Before using this method, test the oil's compatibility with the finish you will apply over it. The oil will blend nicely with most stains, but may discolor a clear-finished piece.

5. How to cut your plywood with a portable circular saw or router

Many of us don't have tablesaws or workshops large enough for ripping full sheets of plywood. What we need: a system for getting good results with portable tools. You can use a router for smooth cross-grain cuts, or a portable circular saw for fast ripping. The edge guide shown *on top of page 59* accommodates both tools. (You can make the guide for use with just one tool, as we did with the

guide shown in the photos *below* and *on page 59*).

Make the ¼" base wide enough so you can trim one side to width

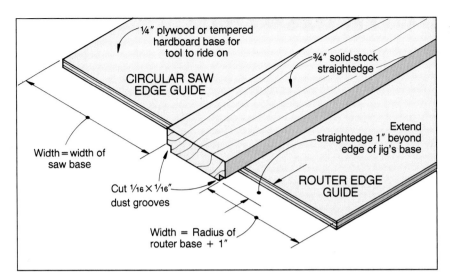

CIRCULAR SAW EDGE GUIDE

¼" plywood or tempered hardboard base for tool to ride on

¾" solid-stock straightedge

Width = width of saw base

Cut ¹⁄₁₆ × ¹⁄₁₆" dust grooves

Extend straightedge 1" beyond edge of jig's base

ROUTER EDGE GUIDE

Width = Radius of router base + 1"

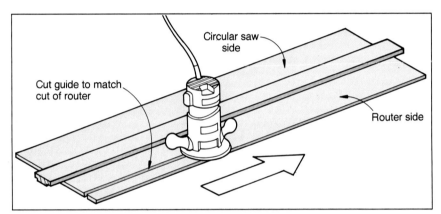

Cut guide to match cut of router

Circular saw side

Router side

Use several 2×2s to make an inexpensive support that prevents you from cutting into your sawhorses.

with your router as shown in the drawing *above center* and the other side with your saw. This way, the router bit or saw blade trims the ¼" base so you can align this edge with the marks on your workpiece

for quick, precise results. We made our edge guide 8' long so it handles almost any plywood job.

You must use the same saw and blade, and the same router and bit, with the guide at all times, so it

helps to write the make and size of these tools on each side of the guide. Otherwise, the edges of the guides will not align with your cutoff marks as required in the the following step.

To make a cut, line up either of the trimmed base edges with your cutoff marks, clamp the edge guide in place, and cut away. As shown in the photo *below left,* we prefer to support the workpiece on top of several 2×2s resting on top of sawhorses.

6. How to get the edge on plywood

Plywood components such as shelves require edging of some sort, and we prefer solid wood over edge banding because of its durability and natural look.

First, glue a ¼"-thick strip of wood onto the edge and trim it as shown *below top.* If you want the edge to look as inconspicuous as possible, trim it to ¹⁄₁₆" thickness as shown *below bottom.*

continued

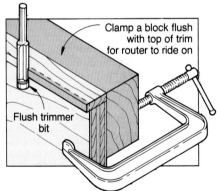

Clamp a block flush with top of trim for router to ride on

Flush trimmer bit

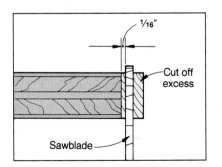

¹⁄₁₆"

Cut off excess

Sawblade

WAYS TO WORK WITH PLYWOOD
continued

7. Getting cornered was never easier

Like edges, plywood corners need disguising. Here's how to handle rabbeted and mitered corners.

For rabbeted corners, glue a ⁵⁄₁₆"-thick trim piece onto the edge of one of the workpieces, and follow the sequence at *right*.

When faced with a mitered corner, we insert a ⅛" spline for increased strength as shown *below left* and *middle*. If the corner doesn't align perfectly, add a ¹⁄₁₆ x ¹⁄₁₆"

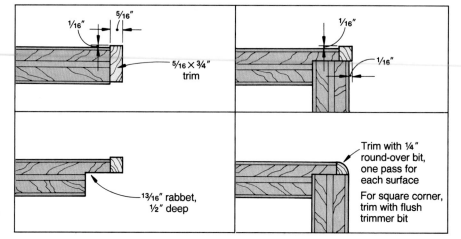

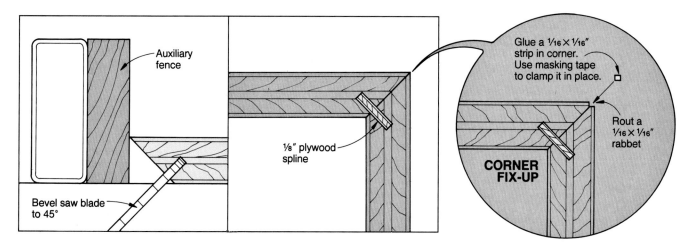

strip as shown in the Detail drawing *above right*. Sand the strip smooth with the surface.

8. To cut dadoes with a router, you need this jig

Routers equipped with straight or spiral bits cut clean dadoes but have one drawback: you can't adjust the bit for different cutting widths. Until now.

With the jig shown *right,* your router, and a single straight bit, you can cut dadoes in widths that range from your bit's width to twice your bit's width. For example, with a ½" bit you can cut dadoes from ½" to 1" wide.

To build the jig, see the drawings and Bill of Materials at *on the next*

page. We sized this jig for routers with 6" bases. If your router has a larger or smaller base, you'll need to change the length of parts B accordingly. The jig will handle

With this jig you can rout tight-fitting dadoes every time.

stock up to 25" wide, but you can make parts A and D longer for larger workpieces.

To use the jig, adjust part D so it's parallel to part A and separated from part A by the width of the router base (place the router base on top of parts B to make this adjustment). Turn the carriage bolts mounted in parts C counter-clockwise until they contact part D.

Now, turn the carriage bolts clockwise as many revolutions as necessary (each revolution equals ¹⁄₁₆") to make up the difference between the width of the straight bit and the width of dado you need. For example, if you need a ¾" dado, and have a ½"-diameter straight bit in your router, back away the carriage bolts ¼" (four revolutions). Mark the carriage-bolt head with a single dot near its rim so you can keep track of the number of revolutions. Now, lock down part D by tightening the nuts that hold it.

For a tight-fitting dado, test your adjustments by making some cuts in scrap stock. Clamp the jig to the scrap stock and feed the router along part A in the direction indicated by the arrows on the jig. After completing this cut, feed the router along part D in the opposite direction. As you enter and exit the cuts, the bit will also cut dadoes in parts B. This won't harm the jig, so long as you don't make cuts deeper than ⅜". If you make a deep cut, replace parts B.

To cut stopped dadoes as we're doing in the photo *on page 60,* just secure the stop block in place by turning its hex-head bolt.

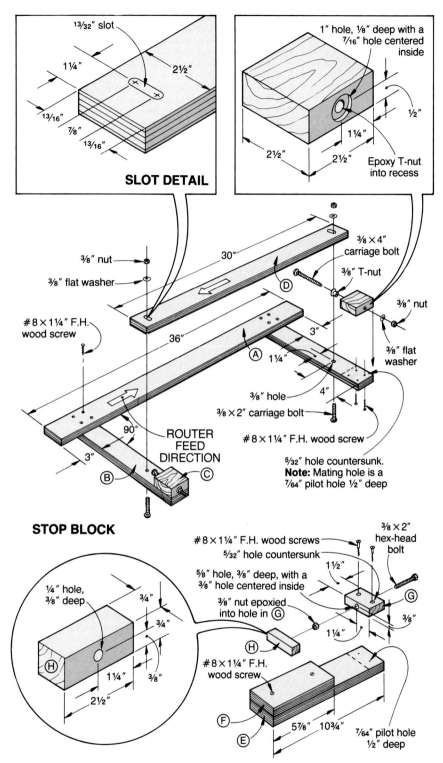

Bill of Materials

Part	Finished Size			Mat.	Qty.
	T	**W**	**L**		
A	¾"	2½"	36"	Plywood	1
B	¾"	2½"	14⅜"	Plywood	2
C	1¹⁄₁₆"	2½"	2½"	Solid stock	2
D	¾"	2½"	10¾"	Plywood	1
E	¾"	2½"	10¾"	Plywood	1
F	¾"	2½"	5⅞"	Plywood	1
G	¾"	1½"	2½"	Solid stock	1
H	¾"	¾"	2½"	Solid stock	1

9. Thin pieces with strength and good looks

Some workpieces—such as fine toy parts or scrollsawed ornaments—have to be thin (¼" or less) *and* strong. The problem: Solid stock won't hold up, and you might not be able to find plywoods in the necessary thickness or species. Even if you can find the right plywood, it's likely to have an inner ply of a contrasting wood. Yuck!

The solution: Cross-laminate several layers of veneer of the same species as shown *on page 62 top.* Apply an even layer of white woodworker's glue between the
continued

WAYS TO WORK WITH PLYWOOD

continued

veneers and secure the sandwich with clamps. After drying overnight, your homemade stock will have strength and good looks.

10. Homemade plywood looks great on cabinetry

The next time you need ¾" plywood with only one good hardwood face, consider laminating ¼"-thick hardwood plywood to a substrate of fir plywood or particleboard. Why? The cost of these materials (plus the necessary glue) usually amounts to less than the cost of a sheet of ¾" hardwood plywood of the same square footage. And, in our trips to lumber outlets, we've often found ¼" plywood (especially oak) that looks far better than what's available in ¾" plywood of the same species.

As shown at *right,* you can make your own plywood by laminating a slightly oversized sheet of ¼" plywood to a substrate (contact adhesive or woodworker's glue will do it). Then, straighten the edges with a flush trimmer bit in your router.

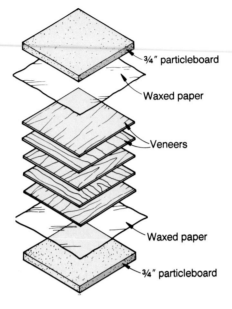

¾" particleboard

Waxed paper

Veneers

Waxed paper

¾" particleboard

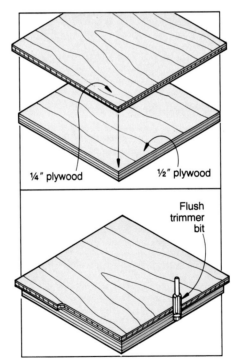

¼" plywood   ½" plywood

Flush trimmer bit

17 Ways to Turn Your Drill Press Into a Shop Hero

In our shop, the drill press earns its keep. We turn to it for help with a myriad of shaping, sanding, boring, cleaning, grinding, and polishing chores. You, too, can test the limits of this truly versatile performer.

We were curious about how many different jobs a drill press can actually do, so we went to work in our shop exploring its uses. Whether the stock is flat or round, small or long, the drill press can handle it. *WOOD* magazine Design Editor Jim Downing even came up with some clever jigs *(see pages 67–68)* to stretch the use of this handy machine even further.

1. Working L-O-N-G

Trying to drill accurate holes near the ends of stock with a standard-size drill press table is a lot like balancing on a high wire. It's a tough job! Here's a solution:

We clamped a piece of ¾" plywood to the drill press table. Make the support as long as necessary, and clamp the work-piece to the fence to keep it from shifting.

2. Get the right angle every time

With our easy-to-make adjustable-angle jig *(see design, page 68)*, you'll never again have to eyeball the angle of cut. To use this jig, just loosen the wing nuts so the fence portion can move freely. Then, use a sliding T-bevel or an adjustable triangle to set the required angle and re-tighten the wing nuts.

continued

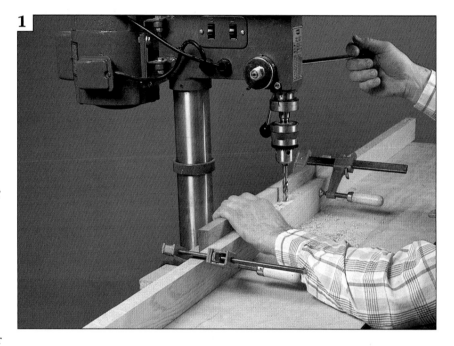

DRILL PRESS
continued

3. Space successive holes perfectly

If you've made a cribbage board, cradle, or other project that calls for drilling hole after evenly spaced hole, you'll appreciate this technique.

To drill a succession of evenly spaced holes, use our "high-low" fence *(see page 68)*. Start by marking the hole spacing on the stock. Center the bit on one of the marks, clamp the stock, and fasten the fence alongside the stock.

Now, pencil a reference mark on the fence, unclamp the stock from the table, and slide the stock along the fence, drilling holes where marked.

For greater accuracy, use a brad-point bit rather than a twist drill. The brad point will produce a straighter hole because it won't skew off course with hard and soft grain.

4. Don't go 'round guessing

You also can use the angle-drilling jig on the previous page to take the guesswork out of drilling round stock, such as a dowel. To be certain you'll drill through the center of the stock, first set the jig at a 45° angle by using a sliding T-bevel as in tip #2. Lower the tip of the bit until it touches the bottom of the jig's V. Clamp the stock to keep it from rolling. Now you're ready to drill the hole. Use a pilot-pointed bit such as a brad-point or Forstner for precise drilling.

5. Getting a handle on small stock

We've had small parts literally fly out of our hands or break apart during drilling, so anytime you can't get a hand on the stock, just clamp it with a handscrew. You'll increase both your control and margin of safety.

Do you want even more control, more safety? Then secure the clamp to the drill press table.

6. Circle cutting the safe way

If you've ever had your fingers smacked by a rapidly spinning circle cutter, you'll appreciate this little tactic. Place the stock against the fence and clamp it with a notched hold-down. Before you start cutting, spin the circle cutter by hand to make sure it clears the fence and hold-down.

In the interest of safety, we painted the ends of the circle cutter yellow for clear visibility.

For best results and less overheating, cut until the pilot drill just penetrates the bottom surface of the stock. Then, turn over the workpiece, put the pilot drill in its hole, and finish the cut.

7. Have a ball drilling spheres

Remember that ball you wanted to attach to a handle on a tool or a favorite toy project? Here's an easy way to put a hole through the center of any sphere.

To start, drill a hole that's somewhat smaller than the ball's diameter into a clamped piece of scrap stock. The secret to this technique is to not change the position of the table or scrap while switching to the desired bit. Place the ball on top of the hole, clamp it, and drill away.

8. Drill holes into ends of dowels

To drill a hole into the end of a short length of dowel, clamp a scrap piece of wood to the table, and drill a hole in it that's the same diameter as the dowel. Without changing the position of the table or scrap piece, change bits and insert the dowel into the hole. Now grab the dowel with a handscrew to keep it from rotating, and drill the centered hole.

9. Make a mighty fine mortise

Even if you don't have a mortising attachment, you can work without one. Lay out the mortise in pencil and center the bit on it. Using a bit of the same width as the mortise, drill the end holes first to control the size of the opening.

With a bit ⅛" smaller than the width of the mortise, bore out the
continued

DRILL PRESS
continued

remaining wood between the holes. You should have a minimum of 1/16" wood on the inside of the edges—enough for hand chiseling up to the edges.

10. Getting "in shape" was never easier

Here, your drill press works like a mini-lathe. You can make your own work arbor from carriage bolts or lengths of all-thread rod.

By using wood rasps, files, sanding blocks, dowels wrapped in sandpaper, or other abrasives, you can shape many small objects.

This photo shows us shaping a pair of drawer pulls, believe it or not. After smoothing on the work arbor, cut the pulls apart as shown.

11. Have big success with small parts

You also can insert one end of the stock directly into the chuck, tightening until the part is firmly held (without crushing the wood). Shape with rasps and successive grades of abrasives.

12. Be a sanding disc jockey

You can save your skin by using a jobber stick like the one shown here. Attach the stick to the workpiece with instant glue or hotmelt glue, and then saw the stick off after you've finished the shaping.

Keep in mind that a slow spindle speed—230 to 700 rpm—gives you the best control when shaping delicate work.

13. Your drum can hum

You just can't top drum-sander attachments for sanding curved edges.

We first cut notches in each side of 1/4" hardboard as shown at *right*. The notches corresponded to the sizes of the common drum sanders. We swung the drill press table off to the side so we could plunge the sander through the cutout in our auxiliary table. With this setup, you'll have less chipping of sanded

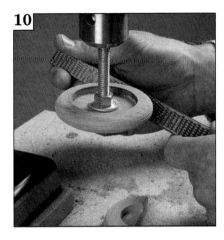

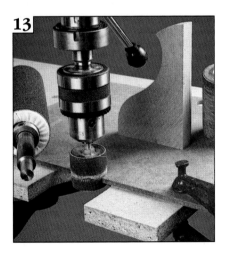

edges as well as edges that are square to the face of the stock.

14. Good-bye, rust. Hello, shiny tool.

Question: How do you turn old tools into new ones?

Answer: With a flap sander, make your tools look like they did when you bought them. With a flip of a switch, you're ready to chase away corrosion on all your tools.

15. Be sharp!

You can quickly sharpen your own jointer/planer blades at home with a handy grinding jig. Now you don't have to take the blades out of your shop and pay someone else to sharpen them, or laboriously do it yourself by hand.

16. Here's a polished performer

Slap a buffing wheel on your drill press and you're ready to clean and polish neglected hardware such as drawer and cabinet handles. Use the buffing wheel in combination with a metal polishing compound to achieve a lustery finish. For best results, run the buffing wheel between 1,500 and 2,000 rpm.

17. Do you know about this clamp?

When a conventional clamp just doesn't do the job, don't forget your drill press. It may offer an effective solution, especially when you're out of other clamps.

Your drill press will enable you to direct pressure from the center of the glued piece, applying the force evenly. This technique is simple; just position the work to be clamped, lower the quill, and tighten the depth stop.

This works great for a variety of applications, especially when you're preparing stock for the lathe. Here, we've attached an auxiliary faceplate to the clamped piece.

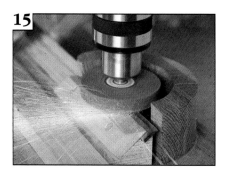

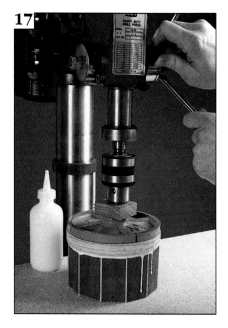

Five tips for better and safer drill press use.

• Don't go off the deep end

Achieving exact depth is easy using the handy technique shown *below right*. Mark the hole depth on the end of the stock, and with the switch off, bring the bit down so its tip aligns with the mark. Lock the drill press depth stop at that point, raise the drill, line the bit up with the marked hole, and proceed.

• Make your flutes play sweet music

Don't place your bit so far into a chuck that you cover the flutes (hollow portion). Covering the flutes may dull the cutting edges and inhibit the bit's ability to remove cuttings when drilling deep holes. Raise and lower bits often to clear flutes of debris, but don't completely clear the top of the hole.

• Avoid chain reactions

To keep track of your chuck key attach it to the side of your drill press with a cord or string. Do not attach it with a chain. If you accidentally turn on the machine with the key inserted, chain links may literally become shrapnel. Always wear adequate face protection when operating a drill press.

• Wear down sanding drums evenly

If you've done a lot of drum sanding on a drill press, you know how a drum tends to wear in one area until you stop sanding to move the drum. The solution: The handy foot pedal shown *above right*. Simply step on the foot pedal to lower the sander. The upward spring-action of the drill press will slowly raise the drum sander as you work.

• Don't lose your temper!

Like people, drill bits lose their temper (hard cutting edge) when caught speeding.

Keep your bits sharp by remembering these points:

• Run larger drill bits slower than smaller bits.

• Drill slower in hardwoods than you would in softwoods.

• Your bit is too hot if water sizzles on its surface. Use water to cool it down.

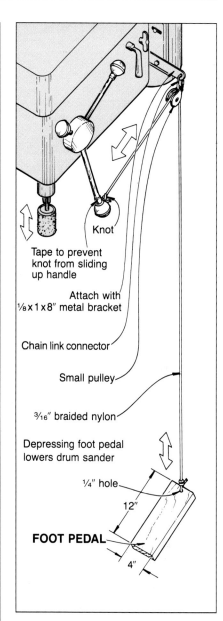

Knot

Tape to prevent knot from sliding up handle

Attach with ⅛ x 1 x 8" metal bracket

Chain link connector

Small pulley

³⁄₁₆" braided nylon

Depressing foot pedal lowers drum sander

¼" hole

12"

FOOT PEDAL

4"

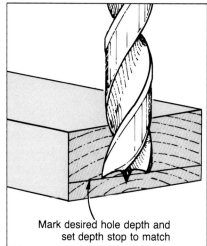

Mark desired hole depth and set depth stop to match

continued

DRILL PRESS

continued

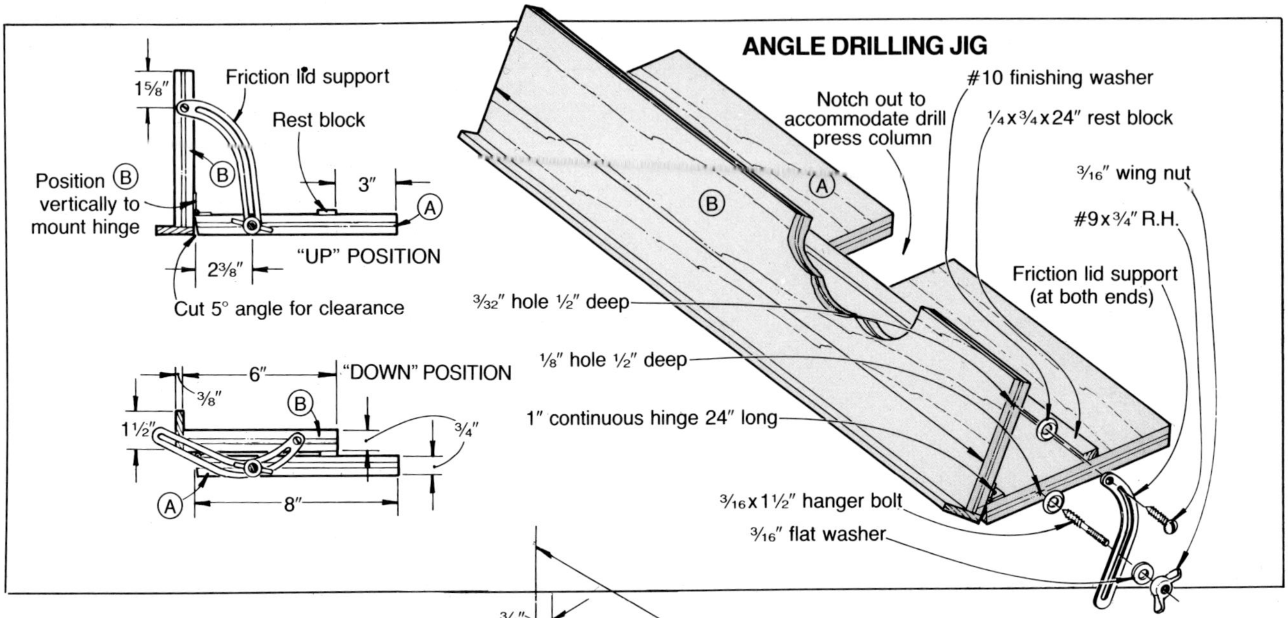
ANGLE DRILLING JIG
Friction lid support
Rest block
1 5/8"
Position Ⓑ vertically to mount hinge
3"
"UP" POSITION
2 3/8"
Cut 5° angle for clearance
6"
3/8"
"DOWN" POSITION
1 1/2"
3/4"
8"
Notch out to accommodate drill press column
#10 finishing washer
1/4 x 3/4 x 24" rest block
3/16" wing nut
#9 x 3/4" R.H.
Friction lid support (at both ends)
3/32" hole 1/2" deep
1/8" hole 1/2" deep
1" continuous hinge 24" long
3/16 x 1 1/2" hanger bolt
3/16" flat washer

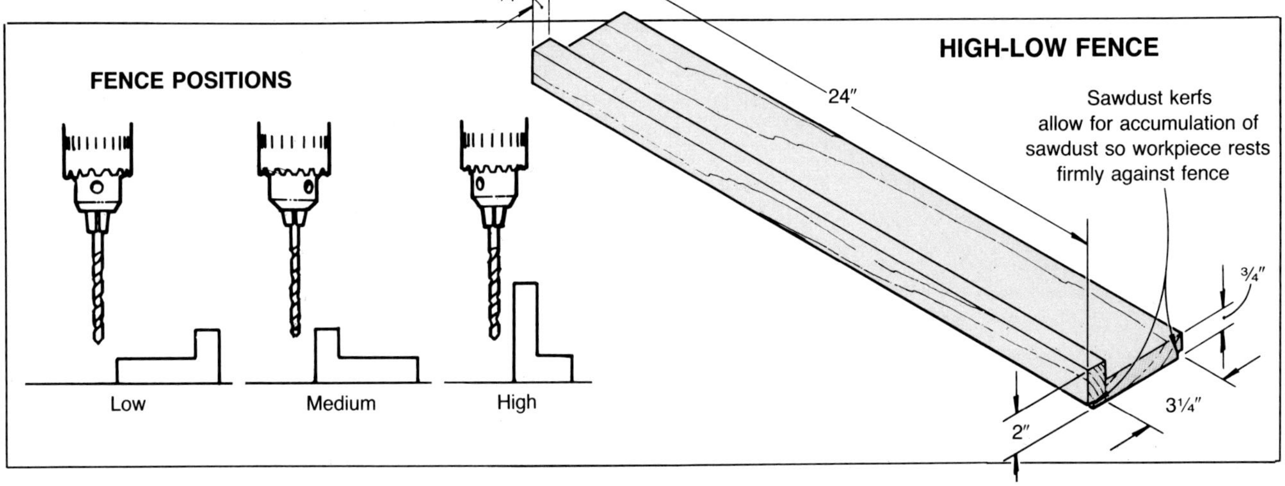
FENCE POSITIONS
Low
Medium
High
HIGH-LOW FENCE
3/4"
24"
Sawdust kerfs allow for accumulation of sawdust so workpiece rests firmly against fence
3/4"
2"
3 1/4"

DRILL PRESS SPEED CHART
Recommended operating speeds (RPM)

Accessory	Softwood (Pine)	Hardwood (Hard Maple)	Acrylic	Brass	Aluminum	Steel	Shop Notes
Twist drills*							
1/16"-3/16"	3000	3000	2500	3000	3000	3000	Lubricate drill with oil when cutting steel 1/8" or thicker.
1/4"-3/8"	3000	1500	2000	1200	2500	1000	
7/16"-5/8"	1500	750	1500	750	1500	600	Use center punch on all holes to prevent drill from wandering.
11/16"-1"	750	500	NR	400	1000	350	
Black & Decker Bullet pilot-point bits*							
1/8"-3/16"	3000	3000	3000	2000	1500	3000	Good all-around bit.
1/4"-3/8"	3000	3000	2400	1500	1000	2000	
1/2"	3000	1500	1600	1500	750	1200	These cut more quickly than brad points and twist drills.
Brad-point bits*							
1/8"	1800	1200	1500	NR	NR	NR	Raise 1/4" and smaller bits often to clear shavings and prevent heat build-up.

Accessory	Softwood (Pine)	Hardwood (Hard Maple)	Acrylic	Brass	Aluminum	Steel	Shop Notes
Brad-point bits* _(continued)_							
¼"	1800	1000	1500	NR	NR	NR	
⅜"	1800	750	1500	NR	NR	NR	
½"	1800	750	1000	NR	NR	NR	
⅝"	1800	500	750	NR	NR	NR	
¾"	1400	250	750	NR	NR	NR	
⅞"	1200	250	500	NR	NR	NR	
1"	1000	250	250	NR	NR	NR	
Forstner bits*							
¼"- ⅜"	2400	700	NR	NR	NR	NR	Raise ¼ - ⅜" bits often to
½"- ⅝"	2400	500	250	NR	NR	NR	clear shavings and prevent
¾"-1"	1500	500	250	NR	NR	NR	heat build-up.
1⅛"-1¼"	1000	250	250	NR	NR	NR	Make several shallow passes with larger bits; allow bit to cool between passes.
1⅜"-2"	500	250	NR	NR	NR	NR	
Multi-spur bits*							
2⅛"-4"	250	250	NR	NR	NR	NR	Smaller sizes also available; use Forstner speeds.
Spade bits*							
¼"-½"	2000	1500	NR	NR	NR	NR	Clamp work to table to improve quality of hole.
⅝"-1"	1750	1500	NR	NR	NR	NR	
1⅛"-1½"	1500	1000	NR	NR	NR	NR	
Irwin Speedbor 2000 bits*							
⅜"-1"	2000	1800	500	NR	NR	NR	Best bit for acrylic Clamp work securely.
Stanley Powerbore bits*							
⅜"-½"	1800	500	NR	NR	NR	NR	Ideal for deep holes and end-grain drilling.
¾"-1"	1800	750	NR	NR	NR	NR	
Circle cutters*							
1½"-3"	500	250	250	NR	NR	NR	Drill one side, flip material over, place center bit in its hole, and resume cut.
3¼"-8"	250	250	250	NR	NR	NR	
Countersinks							
2-flute	1400	1400	NR	NR	NR	NR	Raise and lower frequently for quicker cutting.
5-flute	1000	750	750	250	250	250	
Countersink screw pilot bits							
	2400	250	250	NR	NR	NR	We recommend a slow feed rate.
Taper drill bits with countersinks							
	500	250	250	NR	NR	NR	Clear bit often to prevent heat build-up.
Plug cutters							
	1000	500	NR	NR	NR	NR	
Drum sanders							
Hard rubber	750	1500	750	NR	NR	NR	Avoid load-up and overheating
Soft sleeveless	500	750	750	NR	NR	NR	
3" pneumatic	1750	1750	1750	NR	NR	NR	Decrease air pressure for fine contours.
5" flex discs	750	500	500	500	NR	NR	Adhesive-backed discs work best.
Polishing wheels	1500	1500	1500	1500	2000	NR	Use light pressure.
Flap sander	2000	2000	2000	2000	2000	2400	Hold work firmly.
Grinding wheels	NR	NR	NR	NR	NR	3000	Use 6" or smaller wheel.

NR Not Recommended   *Back material to prevent chip-out   **Always wear a face shield for optimum protection**

Notes • Recommendations are based on visual and tactile tests under shop conditions.   Drilling faster than recommended can cause overheating. Speeds slower than those recommended may cause poor-quality holes. • All testing done on face grain. Reduce speed when drilling into end grain. • Speeds based on new bits from the factory.

DRAWINGS AND PLANS

Drawings and plans
represent a graphic set of
instructions that you use to
build a project. All the lines,
views, dimensions, and
abbreviations form an industry
language that, once understood,
serve as a road map to your
woodworking success.

Reading the draftsman's shorthand

Theoretically, the drawings that
illustrate a woodworking project
should be all the instruction you
need to build that project. The
abbreviations, lines, symbols,
numerals, arcs, and other graphic
devices substitute for words of
step-by-step how-to. The trouble is
many of us haven't been schooled
to understand this special
draftsman's language. See the box
below for commonly used
abbreviations and what they mean.

Dimensions rate as the most
important element in any drawing.
The sketch, *below top,* shows the
many ways draftsmen present
dimensions on their drawings.

Available space usually
determines where the dimension
numbers fall—within the line,
outside the line, or away from it
with an indicator called a *leader.*
There's another style variable you
should know about, too. Those little
delineators on the ends of
dimension lines can assume several
shapes, as shown *below bottom.*

But, regardless of the symbol—
arrowhead, half-arrow, slash, or
dot—they all indicate the distance
between two points.

Radii and angles, shown *below
right,* also appear in different
forms, depending on the draftsman
doing the work. Generally, he or
she will use a consistent style, at
least within the same drawing.

Center lines mark the middle of
parts and the hub of circles, usually
to aid in your dimensioning. As you
can see, *page 71, top left,* they differ
from *hidden lines,* which bring to

your attention those surfaces,
edges, or corners of a part that lie
directly behind the part you're
viewing. Often, you'll be able to
see these parts clearly in another
drawing on the plan.

Assembly lines show you the
relationship of one part to another
in the completed object, such as a
tenon that fits into a mortise; an
arrow indicates the direction of part
movement.

Break lines, illustrated in the
lathe drawings, *page 71, top center,*
represent another often-confused
or misunderstood aspect of draftsman's shorthand. By actually
abbreviating the illustration, they
condense the view of long, uniform
sections or parts. Break lines allow
a draftsman to show you much
greater detail in a drawing that
takes up the same amount of space.
But, just so you always keep the
whole object in mind, you'll always
find total length dimensions used in
conjunction with break lines.

The thick, curved arrows used
in the storage unit section view

DRAFTING ABBREVIATIONS

O.C. = On center
C.C. = Center to center
W/ = With
W/O = Without
I.D. = Inside diameter
O.D. = Outside diameter
O.A. = Overall
~ = Approximately
± ¼" = ¼" tolerance
   either way
¢ = Centerline
TYP. = Typical
   (PARTS THE SAME)
L = Angle
F.H.W.S. = Flat head
   wood screw
R.H.W.S. = Round head
   wood screw

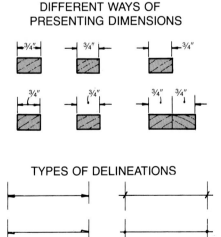

DIFFERENT WAYS OF PRESENTING DIMENSIONS

TYPES OF DELINEATIONS

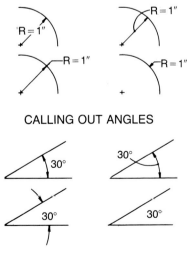

INDICATING RADIUS

$R = 1"$ $R = 1"$
$R = 1"$ $R = 1"$

CALLING OUT ANGLES

30°   30°
30°   30°

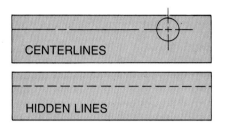

CENTERLINES

HIDDEN LINES

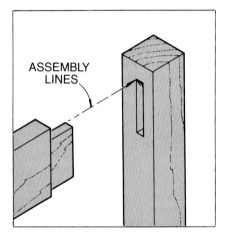

ASSEMBLY LINES

Lathe shown with break lines

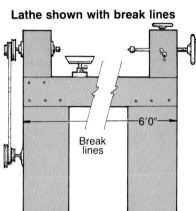

Break lines

6'0"

Lathe shown w/o break lines

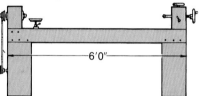

6'0"

COMMON WOODWORKING MATERIALS SYMBOLS

Plywood (as seen on large scale drawings)

Plywood (as seen on small scale drawings)

Solid wood, face or edge grain

Solid wood, end grain

Particleboard or hardboard

Glass or plastic (any shiny surface)

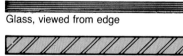

Glass, viewed from edge

Section view of metal

right, signal *part movement.* Where arrows used by themselves might not explain enough, the draftsman will ink in a few brief words of explanation. In our example, the arrows show you which way the cabinet door swings, and the words help you get the picture.

Symbols that identify materials used in the project

Architectural drafting, the kind used for woodworking projects, employs a variety of symbols to represent *materials.* In most woodworking drawings and plans, however, you usually need to recognize only solid wood stock, plywood, composition board, and the other materials shown *above far right.*

Should grain direction be important to the design or

SECTION VIEW OF STORAGE UNIT

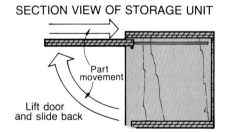

Part movement

Lift door and slide back

construction of the project, you'll see it sketched in as on the illustration for solid wood stock. If critically important to the project's structure, the draftsman will include a notation saying "grain direction" with an appropriate directional arrow. End grain, where it's necessary to be indicated, looks just like the end of a board.

Pictures worth a thousand words

Your eyes see objects in three dimensions—height, width, and depth. When a draftsman attempts to duplicate what your eyes see, he draws an object *pictorially,* using either *isometric* or *perspective* techniques, as shown *on page 72 top.*

You'll most often see isometric drawings on project plans. These pictorial drawings make the object on the paper look three-
continued

DRAWINGS AND PLANS
continued

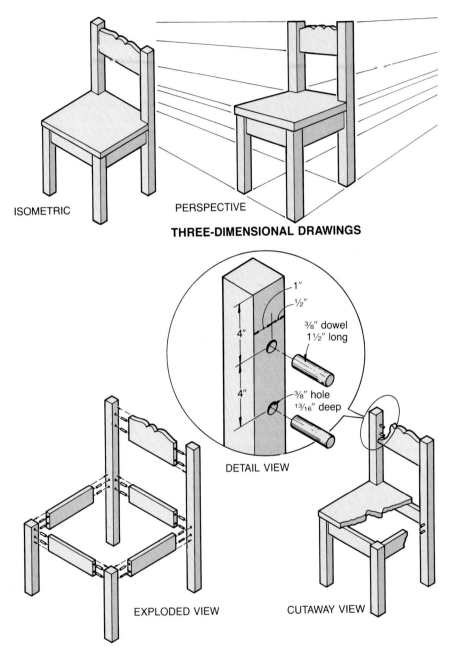

ISOMETRIC   PERSPECTIVE

THREE-DIMENSIONAL DRAWINGS

1"

½"

4"

⅜" dowel
1½" long

4"

⅜" hole
13/16" deep

DETAIL VIEW

EXPLODED VIEW   CUTAWAY VIEW

VIEW DRAWINGS

Many projects are too complicated or have too many parts to be shown with just an exploded view. So, draftsmen sometimes use a *cutaway* view with all the parts intact but some material "cut away" to reveal hidden details.

If necessary, the draftsman will add *detail* drawings to provide you with an enlargement of a specific part or aspect of joinery that otherwise would be difficult to see or comprehend. Actually, exploded, cutaway, and detail views have inherent strengths and weaknesses in the illustration of assembly. That's why they're often used in connection with each other.

Flat-plane drawings do away with the third dimension

Three-dimensional project drawings may look more realistic to you, but for simple, easy to read, easy to transfer dimensions, draftsmen rely on the *orthographic* or *flat-plane* approach.

In flat-plane drawings, you look at the project straight on—usually from the front, the top (sometimes called a *plan* view), or the side. The illustration *opposite, top,* shows you how a draftsman would mentally take a three-dimensional object apart for each view.

A *section* view, shown *opposite, center right,* provides a peek into a project's interior along a single, identified plane, as if the project were sawn in half down that line. By visually sawing it in half, you can see the relationship between the parts in the finished project.

The vertical lines on the front view drawing identify the cut plane from where the view (section A-A) was taken. The short lines with arrowheads indicate the direction you're looking when viewing the section. Section views always show details too complex to depict with hidden lines.

You also can find detail views drawn in the flat plane, *opposite.*

dimensional. If an isometric drawing is done to scale, you could take measurements from it because all parallel lines remain parallel. In perspective, the parallel lines seem to converge at a distant point, like looking down railroad tracks to the horizon. However, most magazine and book drawings are done in perspective. Therefore, you should rely on the dimensions shown. If you find dimensions missing, check the bill of materials.

Draftsmen employ three other pictorial techniques, shown *right,* to help you understand a project. The *exploded view* or *assembly drawing* separates the parts.

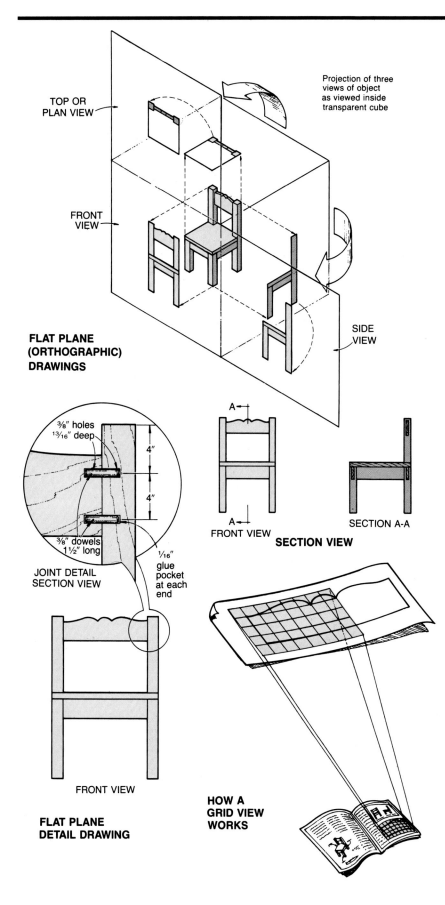

TOP OR
PLAN VIEW

Projection of three
views of object
as viewed inside
transparent cube

FRONT
VIEW

SIDE
VIEW

**FLAT PLANE
(ORTHOGRAPHIC)
DRAWINGS**

3/8" holes
13/16" deep

4"

4"

3/8" dowels
1 1/2" long

1/16"
glue
pocket
at each
end

**JOINT DETAIL
SECTION VIEW**

A→

A→

FRONT VIEW

SECTION VIEW

SECTION A-A

FRONT VIEW

**FLAT PLANE
DETAIL DRAWING**

**HOW A
GRID VIEW
WORKS**

They give you an enlargement of a part, or joinery, that otherwise would be difficult to understand. Dimensions, arrows, and instructions or descriptions support the illustration as necessary.

Project patterns for you to copy

On a project plan, designs or parts with irregular lines, such as a relief carving or a curved chair back, show up drawn as patterns. You can copy *full-size* patterns without reduction or enlargement. But, unfortunately, books and magazines usually can't devote the space needed for full-size patterns, unless the part or design happens to be very small. So, draftsmen use less-than-actual-size patterns called *grid views, below left.*

Drawn on a grid of squares, with each square representing a full-size area, the pattern must be enlarged for you to use it. You'll find the amount of enlargement given as a scale, such as "Each square = 1"." That simply means that you should draw the pattern on paper with 1" squares for faithful reproduction. When a part has two identical halves, only a grid for half the part will be shown, as with the chair back illustrated. You draw the grid view, then cut it out and flip it over for the other half of the part.

REPRODUCING PROJECT PATTERNS

You won't find "gridphobia" listed in Webster's. Medical encyclopedias completely ignore it. But woodworkers feel gridphobia's grip when faced with enlarging a pattern. Their minds freeze at the thought of transposition. Yet, know-how immediately cures the ailment. With photographic technology, it happens in a flash. Even by hand, pattern enlargement becomes child's play.

Due to space limitations, most carving patterns or designs published in magazines, books, and project plans *must* be printed at a reduced size—for you to enlarge. Many woodworkers cringe at

the idea—finding pattern line intersections, placing dots on squares, penciling and erasing— and pass such projects by.

Enlarging isn t difficult, however, and special machines and tools make it even easier. Besides, learning the techniques of pattern enlargement and duplication unlocks unlimited sources of designs—ones gridphobiacs will never see.

Play "follow the dots" with hand enlargement

In publishing, graphic designers reproduce *grids* to illustrate patterns. Those requiring enlargement include the statement *"Each square equals 1" "* (or ½" and

so forth). This notation means that no matter what size grid squares you see in the drawing, you *must* enlarge squares for your full-size pattern to the size indicated.

To use the hand-enlargment method called transposing, you'll need *cross-section graph paper* (the kind with heavier lines marking off each square inch and subdivisions of four or more inner squares), a ruler, an eraser, and a soft-lead pencil. If graph paper isn't available at art, mechanical-drawing, or school-supply stores or at variety retailers, make your own by dividing plain paper into the specified-size squares.

Begin by marking off on your grid paper the same number of

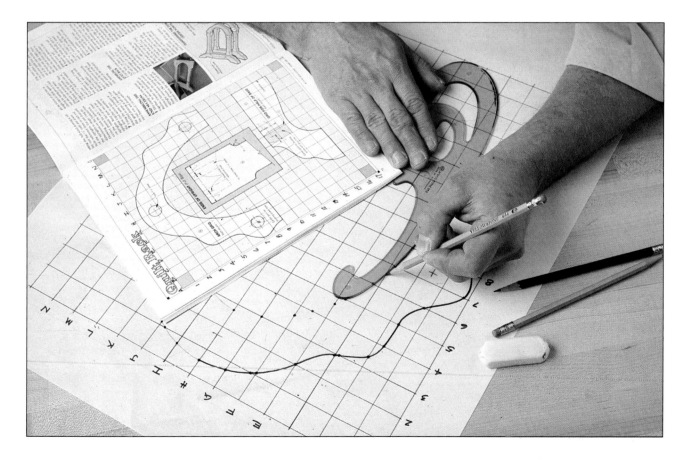

HOW TO TRANSPOSE A PATTERN

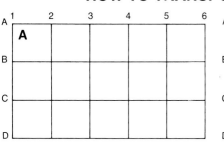

First, number each line in the vertical row. Then, place a letter on each horizontal line.

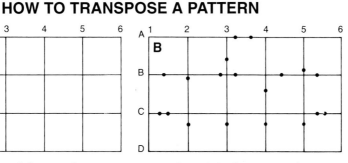

From the original pattern, plot every point where line intersects a square with a dot on your pattern.

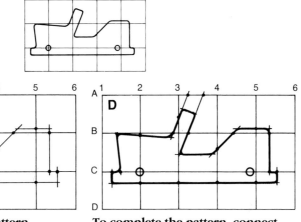

For a more accurate pattern, connect all the straight lines first.

To complete the pattern, connect the dots that represent curves.

TRACING AND TRANSFERRING A HALF-PATTERN

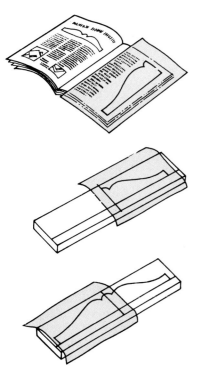

1. Copy the original published pattern onto tracing paper with a soft-lead pencil. Make heavy lines.

2. Flip the pattern over on the board so that it's face down, then again trace over the pencil lines.

3. Lay the pattern down on the other half of the board and again trace over the design to impart pencil lines.

squares as indicated on the pattern grid. Next, number each vertical line in the pattern from left to right and letter each horizontal line from the top down, as in drawing A, *left*. Then, mark the corresponding squares on your graph paper the same way.

Start your pattern enlargement by finding a square on your graph paper that matches the same square on the original. Mark the graph paper grid square with a pencil dot in the same comparative place where a design line intersects a grid line on the original, as shown at *left*. Work only one square at a time. Continue to neighboring squares, marking each in the same way where a design line intersects a grid line.

To avoid discovering any mistakes too late, mark only part of the design, then stop and join the dots with a pencil line. Try to reproduce the original contours as accurately as possible, as in drawing C, *left*. For more precision, draw all straight lines first; then add the curved and angled lines, shown in drawing D, *left*. Once you have transposed part of the design, finish marking the rest of the squares and join those dots in the same way.

Sometimes, as when a pattern repeats itself on the other side of a center line, you'll only have a *half-pattern* to use. To duplicate a full-size half-pattern, copy the original with a soft-lead pencil on tracing paper. Next, flip your traced pattern over and place it pencil-lines-down onto one half of the board. After aligning the pattern for position, go over the pattern lines with your pencil to imprint it on the board. Then, flop the pattern onto the second half of the board and again retrace the pattern to imprint it, as shown in Step 3 in the tracing drawings on the *left*. This method proves faster than copying with carbon paper and doesn't mark up the original pattern.

Push the button and let a machine do the work

In this technological age, a photocopier with enlargement

continued

REPRODUCING PROJECT PATTERNS
continued

capability enlarges a pattern faster and more accurately than transposing. (Not all copiers enlarge, and even some of those that do may be a little inaccurate, so always check your results with a ruler.)

To find out the enlargement percentage you'll need, measure the grid size of the pattern you want to copy. For example, if the pattern grid in the book or magazine measures ½" and the scale calls for 1", you'll need an enlargement twice the size, or 200 percent. A pocket calculator simplifies the mathematics—just divide the number representing the full-size scale by the grid size of the original pattern, then hit the percent (%) key.

Photocopiers have limitations. The ideal photocopier for enlarging patterns—sometimes owned by architectural firms—has the ability to enlarge by 1-percent increments. Some may have only a few sizes of enlargement (or reduction) from which to choose, or have a limit on how large the enlargement can be. With the latter, you can still make a full-size pattern by enlarging it in two steps.

For instance, the photocopier's enlargement limit might be 150 percent and you need a 200 percent enlargement. So, first make an enlargement of the original to the 150-percent limit. Then, using a calculator, divide your desired size of 200 by your enlargement limit of 150 percent (200 divided by 150). Your answer will be 133 percent.

Next, set the machine to copy at 133 percent and enlarge the pattern you already made at 150 percent. Your final pattern will be 200 percent larger than the original.

Patterns by projection—
just like school

A few machines enable you to quickly and accurately enlarge a pattern. Typically, they're not found at home, but available (for a fee)

from libraries, schools, and audiovisual rental companies.

An *opaque projector* accepts flat, horizontal artwork and projects it

onto a vertical surface, such as a screen or a wall. Enlarge or reduce a pattern by taping a graph-paper grid to the wall. Place the original

A mechanical tool to toy with

With a device called a *pantograph,* you can enlarge (or reduce) patterns at your desktop or workbench. Looking very much like the expandable, protective gate used to keep toddlers from tumbling down a stairwell, a pantograph consists of an arrangement of hinged arms. After you adjust the device for the enlargement needed, you outline the original pattern with the stylus, or tracing end. While you trace the lines with the stylus, the pantograph's pencil end draws the enlargement. It's as simple as that.

Although pantographs usually have an enlargement capability up to 8:1, you'll get sharper reproduction if you stick to a limit of 4:1 (400 percent). If you don't, you'll find yourself working in a tiny area

with the stylus while the pantograph's fully extended pencil arm flaps about. To enlarge greater than 4:1, do it in two steps. That is, for an 8:1 enlargement, use the pantograph to first make a 4:1 enlargement. Then, again enlarge the pattern 2:1.

In setting up the pantograph on your worktable or drawing board, be sure to affix the original pattern and the copy sheet close enough to each other so that the arms won't spread excessively (see photo, *below*). Be sure, also, to tighten all the pantograph fittings. Any looseness creates wobbly, floppy arms and inaccurate tracing.

You can buy a pantograph at art supply stores.

To avoid wobble, which results in inaccurate reproduction, don't spread the pantograph's arm too wide. Tighten all fittings, too.

Finding proportions with dividers

Proportioning dividers, available at drafting-supply stores, enable you to accurately enlarge even a tiny section of a pattern, such as a fractional line or other detail. However, this tool won't draw the segment for you.

Dividers perform solely as a measuring device. First, you measure the length of a line on the original pattern with the points on one end of the dividers. By setting the enlargement size, the points on the opposite end will automatically extend themselves to the enlarged size. To transfer the measurement to the enlargement, simply flip ends of the dividers (see photos, *below*). With proportioning dividers, you can transfer minute details.

One end of proportioning dividers measures the dimension of a detail on the original.

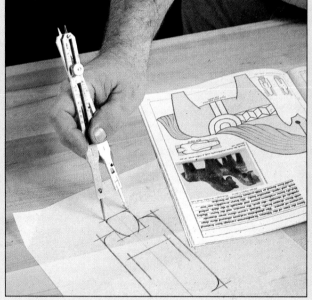

The other end translates the original dimension to the exact scale you choose for the reproduction.

pattern in the projector, and then line up its projected squares on your wall-mounted paper grid. Keep moving the projector back and forth to the wall until the grids line up. When they do, pencil in the projected lines.

An *overhead projector* receives transparent material in the form of a clear acetate sheet, and projects the image onto a screen or wall. An overhead projector operates in the same way as an opaque projector, except that you must trace the lines of the original pattern onto the clear acetate with a non-smearing, felt-tip marking pen before projection.

The printing, publishing, and advertising industries enlarge artwork with huge cameras. The same method works perfectly for enlarging patterns. For a few dollars you can purchase a correctly sized *reproduction stat* ("stat"), a black-and-white photo print of the original that provides accurate detail. You simply request that the print be made to the exact size you want. Check the Yellow Pages under "Photostatic Copy Service" or "Photo Copying." Sometimes, fast-service print shops offer reproduction stats, too.

WOODWORKERS' STANDARDS FOR SEATING

It's no accident that standard kitchen countertop height is 36", that 5/4 lumber measures 1 1/16" thick when dried and surfaced, and that the correct backrest angle for dining ranges from 0° to 5° to the rear. These and a host of other standards have been established over the years by the furniture and wood industries, and by designers. Here we'll summarize the data, starting with seating, then the standards for tables, shelving and cabinets.

Louis Sullivan once said, "Form follows function," and this design principle holds especially true in seating. Before considering form—that is, style, scale (or how it relates in size to its surroundings), wood species, or joinery techniques—you must consider comfortable support of the human body.

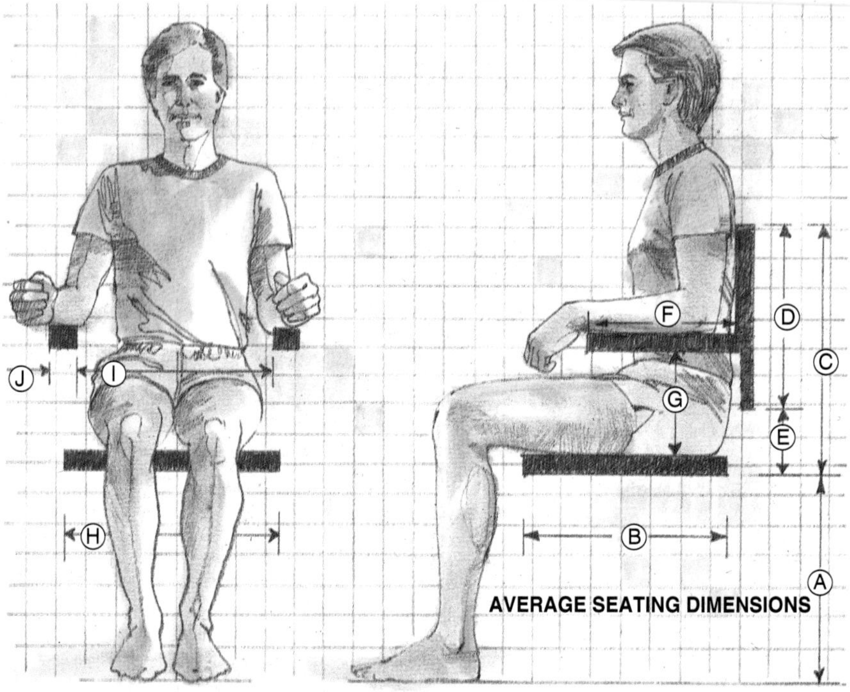

AVERAGE SEATING DIMENSIONS

Average seating dimensions

The design of a comfortable chair depends on the size and shape of the person it's intended to support. So use the dimensions listed at *right* only as what they are intended to be—guidelines. You may need to adjust them slightly for your situation, and that's fine.

Seating angles

You've no doubt noticed that the angle of seating varies from one type of seating to another. Here again, it's function that dictates. *We've categorized all seating into three groupings: Alert, Relaxed, and Reclining.* In the box at the top of the opposite page, we discuss how these postures govern the angles that are right for a given piece of furniture.

AVERAGE DIMENSIONS*

		ADULT	9 yrs.	7 yrs.	5 yrs.
A	Seat height	16¾"	12¾"	11½"	10½"
B	Seat depth	15½"	11¾"	10¾"	9¾"
C	Backrest height	15"	11"	10¼"	9¾"
D	Backrest	12"	5⅜"	5⅛"	5"
E	Seat to backrest	3" min.	5⅝"	5⅛"	4¾"
F	Armrest length	8⅜" min.	6"	6"	6"
G	Armrest height	8"	6⅝"	6⅛"	5¾"
H	Seat width	16-20"	13"	12"	11"
I	Armrest spacing	18½" min.	14"	13"	12"
J	Armrest width	2" average for all ages			
K	Backrest width	16-18"	11" min. for 9 thru 5		

*All dimensions are for alert posture (dining, writing, etc.). Adult dimensions are for the average American male. Seating designed for the typical American female should be downsized somewhat.

If you use cushions, adjust the dimensions so they are correct when the cushion is compressed by the weight of the occupant. As a rule of thumb, you can deduct half the cushion thickness from the seat height (A).

HOW FUNCTION DICTATES THE SEATING ANGLE

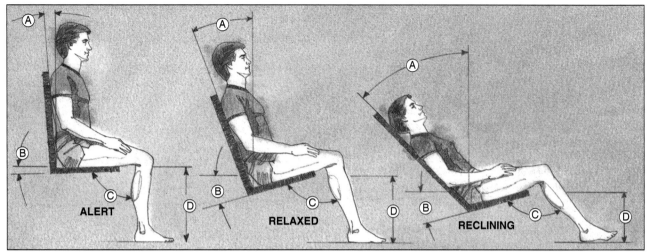

ALERT

RELAXED

RECLINING

Alert *dining, writing*
• Quite often, the back of the chair runs straight up and down (0°), but it may have a back angle up to 5° to the rear (A).
• Generally, you'll want the back of the seat lower than the front edge. In the instance *above,* the angle measures 5°; this is fairly typical (B).
• The seat height (C) determines the knee bend angle (D) For dining, the knee bend angle is normally 90°, with an average seat height of 16¾".

Relaxed *conversation, TV, reading*
• To lean back and relax, you want to factor in a back angle (A) of between 10° and 30°.
• With the back angled this way, you have to angle the seat upward slightly to keep a person from sliding out of the chair. The seat angle (B) ranges from 5° to 10°.
• You always want the knee bend angle (C) to be between 90° and 100°. To accomplish this in the example *above,* you need to decrease the seat height (D) from the standard 16¾" to 15½", which moves the heel forward.

Reclining *lounging, resting*
• Back angle (A) varies considerably from piece to piece, but never exceeds 55° to the rear. When it's greater than 30°, you have to provide support for the head. To do this, increase the distance from the seat to the top of the back to at least 32".
• The seat angle (B) ranges from 10° to 15° for lounging purposes.
• You want the knee angle to be from 100° to 120°. We accomplished this above by decreasing the seat height to 14". This again moves the heel forward.

Dining chair

When entertaining, many people consider the dining table the center of activity. So you want to plan as much comfort into dining chairs as possible. Seat cushions help ensure a comfortable stay. We think that a simple foam cushion on plywood makes good sense in most situations. Figure on a 2" cushion being about average.
• The seat height of most dining chairs measures about 16¾"

including the compressed height of the seat cushion.
• Armrests on a dining chair add to the comfort factor, too. Most designers plan on a maximum arm height above the seat of 8". But don't forget about the apron height of the table you're planning to use the chair with. You want to make sure the arms will slide under the apron. In any event, you wouldn't want the armrest height less than 6".

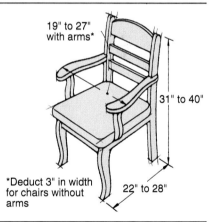

19" to 27" with arms*

31" to 40"

*Deduct 3" in width for chairs without arms

22" to 28"

Dinette chair

Compared to dining chairs, dinette chairs are often smaller in scale, mainly because of the limited size of most areas they occupy.
• Normal seat height averages 16¾" and that includes the height of the seat cushion, if used.
• The overall depth of the chair may be as little as 15½" up to a maximum of 20". And the width

ranges from 16" to 18", depending on the style of chair being constructed.
• The style of furniture largely dictates the back height. A low-slung Padova chair, for example, has a back height of only 13½" above the seat, but a ladder-back chair may be as high as 23½".

continued

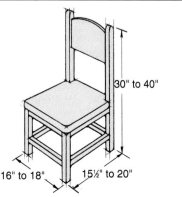

30" to 40"

16" to 18"   15½" to 20"

STANDARDS FOR SEATING

continued

Easy chair

Chairs designed for relaxing typically have a lower seat height than those for dining or study. The seat tips back to a greater degree front to back, and the seat back angle increases, too.

• Seat height averages 16" and angles front to back at about 10° With easy chairs, the seat cushion may be quite thick, so be sure to allow for cushion compression when figuring seat height.

• Because the seat is low and angled back, armrests aid in getting into and out of the chair. Typically, they rise 5" to 8" above the seat and measure between 2" and 4" wide.

• This chair's seat back, angled back about 10°, rises 15" above the cushion. Some high-back wing chairs, though, have backs as high as 33".

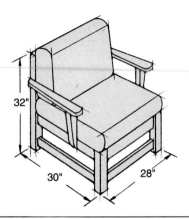

Sofa

• Seat depth varies, depending on the thickness of the back cushions, but 18" to 22" is a good place to start.

• The back, typically 17" above seat height, usually angles back at least slightly, but can do so up to 25°.

• The armrests most often rise up from 4" to 8" above the highest point of the seat cushion.

• In figuring the width of a sofa, allow 24" per person, plus 4" to 6" for each armrest.

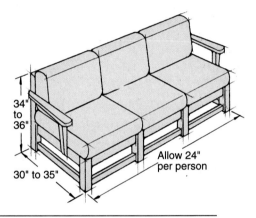

Bar stool

A bar stool, obviously, must fit the bar with which it's used. Average bar height runs from 40" to 44". Whatever its height, you want the seat to be from 12" to 15" below the top surface of the bar, but never higher than 30".

• Bar stools average about 16" to 18" square, or 16" to 17" in diameter if you go with a round seat. Overall dimensions at the base rarely exceed 18" square.

• The top of the seat back is normally 11" or 12" above the cushion. And since people tend to lean forward when sitting in a bar stool, be sure to leave at least 3" between the bottom of the back and the top of the seat for the person to expand into.

• And don't forget to provide for a place to hang your heels. A rung 20" below the top of the seat works nicely for this.

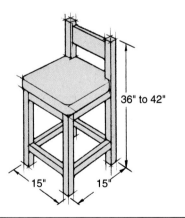

Outdoor lounge

Three elements combine to create the overall length of 72"— the leg rest, seat, and backrest. The leg rest measures 22" long and is designed to support the leg from the knee down. It raises along with the seat, creating a knee-bend angle of 120°.

• Seat depth averages 17" and can be inclined up to 10°.

• Backrest height typically measures 33". You can adjust its angle backward from 45° to the flat bench position.

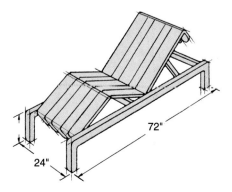

WOODWORKERS' STANDARDS FOR TABLES

When you set out to design a table, you already know what function you want it to serve. But you also need to select a style that will complement the other furnishings in your home.

Choosing a style and support system

If you're unsure about which style to choose, stop by some furniture showrooms and browse a bit. Be sure to take along a pad of paper, a pencil, and a tape measure so you can record overall dimensions.

Also take a look at how the table you like is supported. The drawing at right gives you a preview of your options. *Leg/apron-supported tables,* the most popular traditional type, depend on a well-constructed leg/apron assembly for their stability.

Trestle-base tables, a favorite of Early American craftsmen, have two end legs with spread feet connected by a center support member that's usually near floor level. The support structure usually goes together with "through

Trestle base support

Pedestal base support

Leg/apron support

mortise-and-tenon" joints, and are held secure with a wedge, which you can remove for easy disassembly.

The framework beneath *pedestal-base tables* can take several shapes.

Some have a single pedestal with four feet at the base. Others have two smaller pedestals that connect to a split base. And a more contemporary version features a single cylinder without legs.

The relationship between tables and chairs

Any time you pull a chair up to a table or desk, the two must be sized correctly or you won't be comfortable. Keep these pointers in mind as you are designing:

• Most dining tables and study desks have a height (A) of 29".

• The average American male needs a leg space of 25" from the floor to the apron bottom (B).

• Keep the top of the chair seat about 12" to 13" below the top surface of the table (C). Figure in cushion compression (half the cushion thickness) if you use one.

• If possible, plan a 24" foot space (D) between the edge of the table and the support assembly. With pedestal tables, 18" is all you can get and still have a sturdy surface.

• Make sure the armrest height (E) allows you to slide the chair in under the apron of the table.

• When designing juvenile furniture, plan on a tabletop height of 22½" for 9-year-olds, 21½" for 7-year-olds, and 20" for 5-year-olds. And keep the top of the chair seat about 10" below that.

continued

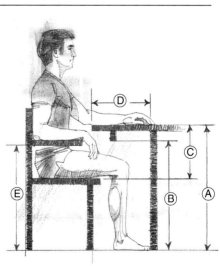

STANDARDS FOR TABLES
continued

Style of entertaining affects dining table size

You've all been in dining situations where it seemed that you couldn't make a move without knocking into someone else's elbow or leave the table without having to ask someone to move their chair. These and other space problems can be solved while the table is still on the drawing board.

The drawing at *right* shows how your style of entertaining impacts directly on the space needed to accommodate a group for a meal. Casual dining requires less space, mainly because of the lesser amount of dinnerware used.

When determining the width and length of dining tables, keep these factors in mind:

• Allow a 12" by 24" space for each casual place setting. For formal tables, figure 15" by 28" each.

• Figure in a space of 12" wide and as long as possible to serve as a serving space.

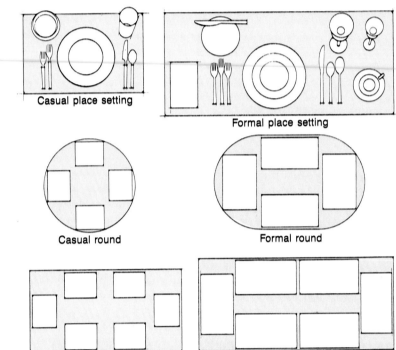

Casual place setting

Formal place setting

Casual round

Formal round

Casual rectangular

Formal rectangular

Rectangular trestle table

Trestle-design tables have been a favorite of designers for centuries. They're rugged, practical, and fit in well with Early American and country furnishings.

• Make sure that you position the legs at least 18" in from the ends of the table to provide adequate foot space for the host and hostess.

• The table shown here, a typical example, measures 38" wide, 70" long, and 29" high. Though not many trestle tables extend, on this one, the ends pull out and accept up to two 15" leaves for a total length of 100".

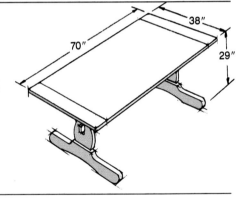

Round pedestal dining table (extension type)

This table measures 48" in diameter and can extend up to 78". As the tabletop is pulled apart, the pedestal comes apart. This type of table affords you more strength and stability when extended than one with a single base.

• When designing the base, be sure to allow for foot space. Notice how the cutouts between the feet of this table provide adequate clearance .

• Another type of pedestal table, the cylinder-base table, typically measures 48" in diameter with an 18" base, which allows for leg room and sufficient stability. You can add sand to the base, if desired.

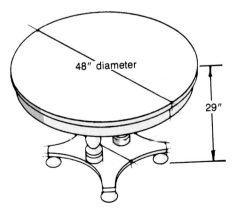

Drop-leaf extension table

This style of table continues to be popular, and ease of use and the space-conserving nature could be the reasons why. These tables function especially well in areas too small for other, more bulky options. And they adapt quite nicely to use as either a dining table or a coffee table.

• This table measures 23" wide and 42" long with the leaves down, but with the leaves up it measures 42" in length.

• Drop-leaf tables such as the one shown here are supported at each corner by a leg/apron support structure that provides exceptional stability.

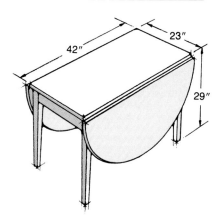

Coffee table

Though the shapes and sizes of these tables vary considerably, height remains fairly constant at between 16" and 17". It should approximate the height of the sofa seat, perhaps an inch or two taller. This table measures 22" wide, 60" long, and 16" high.

• Widths vary from 19" to 27" and lengths range from 36" to 60" depending on the length of your sofa. Figure on the coffee table being anywhere from ½ to ⅔ the length of the sofa.

• Round and square tables range in size from 36" to 42" across.

• You may want to build in some storage or display space beneath the surface of the table, as in the example shown here.

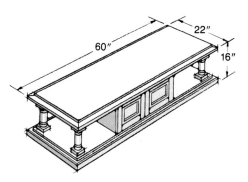

End table

For an end table to function as it should, it must be at the same height or a few inches lower than the armrest height of the sofa it sits next to. If you plan to set a lamp on the table, adjust the height so the bottom of the lampshade equals the eye height when seated.

• Most end tables are rectangular in shape and range in width from 22" to 24" and from 24" to 28" deep. Hexagonal and square tables typically measure from 24" to 28" across.

• Depending on the table support system you choose, you may be able to incorporate some storage space in the design.

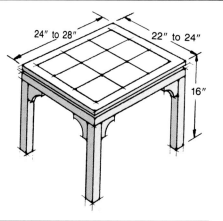

Sofa table

Sofa tables, those stately furniture pieces designed to sit behind a sofa, usually stand from 26" to 27" high, depending on the height of the sofa back.

• These tables' main function is to conceal the back side of sofas that are not against a wall. As a result, most often, they're quite narrow—from 14" to 17" wide.

• Sofa tables average 60" in length again depending on the length of the sofa. Good scale calls for a sofa table that's approximately ⅔ the length of the sofa.

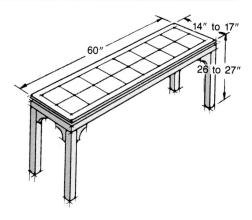

WOODWORKERS' STANDARDS FOR BOOKCASES & SHELVES

Libraries make the most of every inch of shelf space. Careful calculations of book size and weight make it possible to store vast collections. When it's time for you to build storage at home, your audiovisual equipment, books, and collectibles demand no less attention.

Bookcases and shelves begin with planning, not only for stability and attractiveness, but because the size and spacing of your shelves will be determined by what you'll put on them. Down at your local library, for instance, the staff knows that every running foot of shelf space will hold 10–12 children's books, or seven fiction titles, or five medical books. For your home library, you may not need to be quite so exacting, but glancing at the chart *below* you'll see that all books and audiovisual equipment —for purposes of shelf spacing— aren't created equal.

ITEM	HEIGHT BETWEEN SHELVES	SHELF DEPTH
Children's books	8"	8"
Paperbacks	8"	10"
General reading	11"	12"
Large hardbound	15"	12"
Reference	10"	14"
Magazines	10–12"	14"
Record albums	13¼"	14"
Slide trays	9¾"	10"

If you plan to house your television, stereo, speakers, and other entertainment equipment in the same shelving unit, you'll need a shelf depth of from 18" to 20" for most systems and a height spacing made to order for your components. Videocassettes (about 1x9x6"), audiocassettes (½x3x4") and compact discs (½x5½x5") can fit into custom or ready-made racks, either on shelves or in drawers. When shelving units accommodate audiovisual components as well as books, they often are in modular sections: a deeper one for the bulkier equipment, and side or top bookcase/display units.

The goal: sagless spans

For traditional, living-room-type storage, shelving options include glass. acrylic, and wood. Each type of material, however, has a span limit—the maximum distance it can span between supports without sagging or breaking under a load. Architects figure that books represent a load averaging 25 pounds per cubic foot. The chart *below* indicates the maximum, no-sag span limit (under load) of the most commonly used shelving materials.

MAXIMUM NO-SAG SPAN WITHOUT ADDITIONAL SUPPORT

MATERIAL	MAXIMUM SPAN
¾" plywood	36"
¾" particleboard	28"
¾" hardwood board*	48"
½" acrylic	22"
⅜" glass	18"

*Wood species vary in rigidity

Most solid hardwood shelves are stiffer than plywood or other materials, but as noted above, this varies with the species. Here's how some common hardwoods stack up:

Stiff—aspen, alder, butternut, poplar

Stiffer—ash, cherry, mahogany, walnut

Stiffest—beech, birch, maple, oak, pecan

You can increase the stiffness of a wood shelf by sinking screws into the shelf through the solid back of the case. For more strength, attach a 1x2" cleat to the front of the shelf, or to the front and the back, as in the drawing *below*. Or, you can build an amazingly strong, yet lightweight shelf called a *torsion box*. When constructed as shown *below*, a 1½ x 12" torsion box shelf using oak-faced plywood has two-thirds less deflection under weight than ¾ x 12" solid oak at one third the cost.

Only dust collects on shelves you can't reach

In a hallway, mudroom, family room, or bedroom, shelves usually store more than books. This means that gloves, hats, boots, toys, and other frequently used items have to be within reach of family members. Follow these guidelines for easy-to-reach shelf heights:

AGE	SHELF HEIGHT MAXIMUM
Preschoolers	4'
Through third grade	4' 3"
4th through 6th grades	4' 7"
Young teens	5' 1"
Adults	5' 8"

Putting shelves in their place permanently

Permanently attaching shelves to the sides (vertical supports) adds strength and rigidity to a shelving unit or cabinet. The drawing, *right*, shows the most common methods. Wooden *cleats* attached to the vertical supports provide a resting place for shelving and are the easiest, but not always the most attractive solution. When glued and screwed to the shelf as well as the sides, cleats provide stout support.

The *dado* offers a stronger, cleaner-looking alternative to the cleat. Tightly fitted and glued into

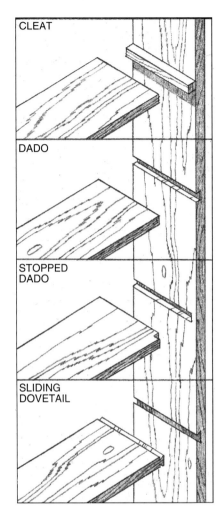

OPTIONS FOR FIXED SHELVES

CLEAT

DADO

STOPPED DADO

SLIDING DOVETAIL

the dado, the shelf unites with the wood all along the cut for tough support. Many woodworkers cover the exposed dado end with a strip of matching wood or veneer tape.

Going the dado one better, the *stopped dado* doesn't need to be concealed with veneer tape or a wood strip. However, cleaning out the dado and notching the shelf for a tight, no-rattle fit requires some skill and effort.

Choose *sliding dovetails* for truly decorative shelf support joints. Besides their attractiveness, sliding dovetails resist racking and provide the strongest joint because the shelf and the case side interlock.

continued

TECHNIQUES TO INCREASE SPAN

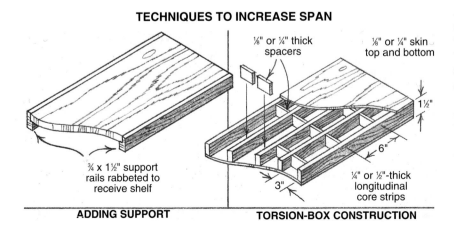

⅛" or ¼" thick spacers

⅛" or ¼" skin top and bottom

1½"

6"

¾ x 1½" support rails rabbeted to receive shelf

3"

¼" or ½"-thick longitudinal core strips

ADDING SUPPORT   **TORSION-BOX CONSTRUCTION**

STANDARDS FOR BOOKCASES & SHELVES
continued

When you can't make up your mind

Adjustable shelves allow you to alter spacing to suit changing lifestyles and whims for display. As this option grows in popularity, new types of hardware continue to be developed. We show the basic alternatives for installing adjustable shelves *below*.

Eliminating the need for any hardware, the wooden *bar-and-notch* method has been used for at least a hundred years. Wedge-shaped notches cut at regular intervals into 1×2s attached to the unit's sides accept wooden bars to support shelves. Note also that you must notch the corners of each shelf to fit against the sides. You won't be able to make small changes in shelf spacing, but for a refurbished antique or reproduction piece, the bar and notch system looks authentic.

Pin supports, made from metal or plastic, fit into ¼" holes drilled in the sides of the unit. This method permits more flexibility in spacing, but requires super-accurate drilling for perfectly level shelves. Also, because of the L-shaped design of most pins, shelves won't butt tightly against the sides. Using hardwood dowels instead of pins eliminates these gaps, but unless you cut grooves in the bottom of the shelf to accommodate the dowels, this method appears rustic.

Metal and plastic *standards and clips* install easily and accurately. You can surface-mount the support strips on the case sides. To avoid space at the ends of the shelves recess the vertical strips in shallow dadoes.

A relatively new, practically invisible, shelf support from Sweden features a *spring steel clip.* To attach them, you saw a blind slot in the ends of each shelf to conceal the clip. The ends of the wire clip fit into 5/32" holes you drill in the shelf sides.

Wrestling with rack and wobble

Stand two boards on end, then fasten to them a top board and a bottom one, and you have the basic bookcase: two uprights and two shelves. You can use corner joinery such as the *rabbet* and the *dado,* detailed *above right,* to make strong, good-looking joints.

Installing fixed shelves helps stiffen the construction, but they won't necessarily eliminate wobble.

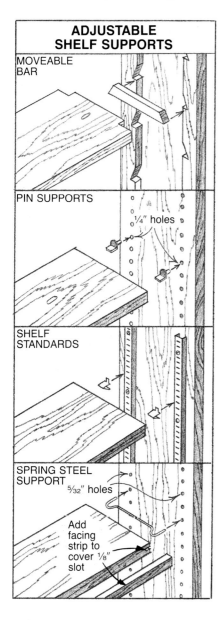

ADJUSTABLE SHELF SUPPORTS

MOVEABLE BAR

PIN SUPPORTS
¼" holes

SHELF STANDARDS

SPRING STEEL SUPPORT
5/32" holes
Add facing strip to cover 1/8" slot

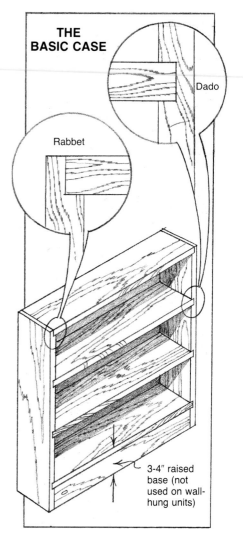

THE BASIC CASE

Dado

Rabbet

3-4" raised base (not used on wall-hung units)

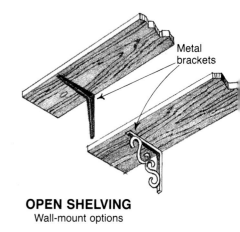

Metal brackets

OPEN SHELVING
Wall-mount options

SOLUTIONS TO RACK AND WOBBLE PROBLEMS

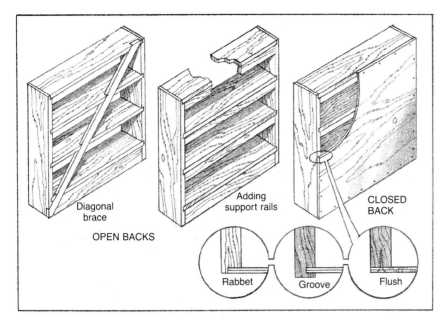

Diagonal brace

OPEN BACKS

Adding support rails

CLOSED BACK

Rabbet

Groove

Flush

HOW TO DEAL WITH BASEBOARDS

Cut cardboard template to fit baseboard profile. Using template as a guide, cut case side or upright to fit.

Reduce width of lowest shelf, if necessary

Bottom shelf covers existing baseboard

Notch shelf upright to fit over baseboard

Make new baseboard to match existing

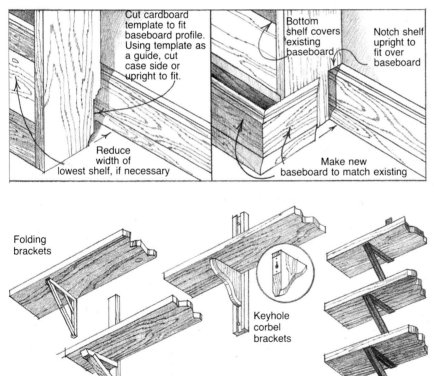

Folding brackets

Wood bracing

Keyhole corbel brackets

Z brackets

Fastening the basic case to a wall quickly sturdies it. A freestanding unit, however, calls for one of the solutions demonstrated at *left*. The simplest way to steady a wobbly case: the unattractive, but effective *diagonal brace*. For a better-looking alternative, attach *support rails* to the shelf bottoms and the case back.

Mounting a solid back *flush* to a case offers about the same stability as wall attachment, if you glue and screw the back to each member. Other back-joining options include the *rabbet* and the *groove*. To use this technique, cut a groove into both sides and the top and bottom. Then fit a plywood or hardboard back into the groove. A face frame added to the front of the case will also strengthen it.

A freestanding shelving unit poses another problem, especially in older homes: How do you set it tight against a wall when there's a baseboard molding? You'll find two solutions to the problem.

Shelves in a hurry

Open shelving, often referred to as "utility" shelving because it dutifully fulfills the storage role in basement, laundry room, or garage, can dress up and look presentable for company, too. Use keyhole corbel brackets and those made to resemble wrought iron scrollwork for a more decorative look. These, as well as the other types of brackets, *left,* allow you to set up open shelving quickly, and change shelf spacing when the whim hits you.

If your open shelving system has to bear heavy loads, you'll have to attach the standards (or brackets alone, in some cases) to the wall with sturdy hardware, such as lag screws set directly into wall studs. Hollow-wall anchors and toggle bolts will handle only light loads in wallboard or plaster and lath.

WOODWORKERS' STANDARDS FOR KITCHEN CABINETS

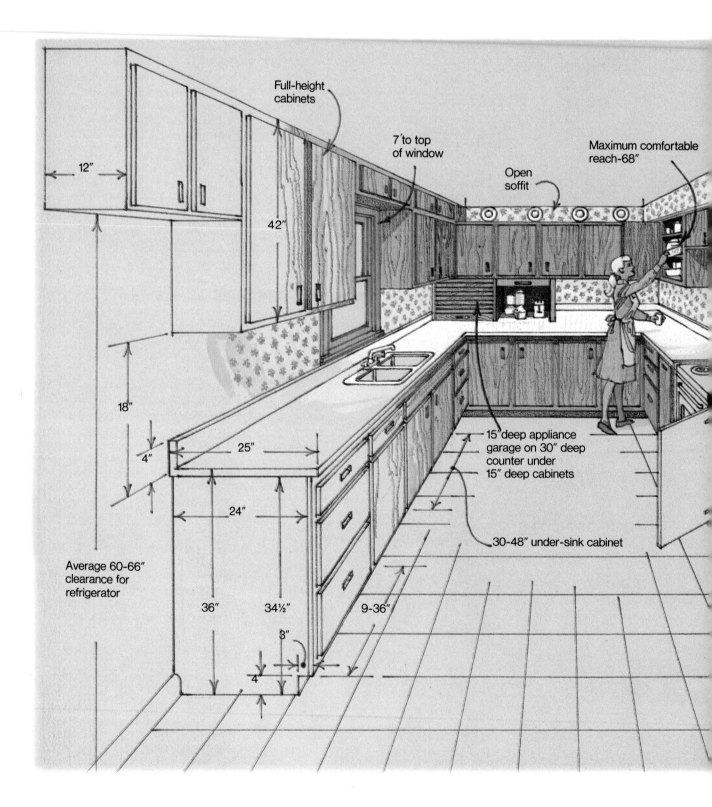

Full-height cabinets

7' to top of window

Open soffit

Maximum comfortable reach-68"

12"

42"

18"

4"

25"

24"

36"

34½"

9-36"

3"

4"

Average 60-66" clearance for refrigerator

15" deep appliance garage on 30" deep counter under 15" deep cabinets

30-48" under-sink cabinet

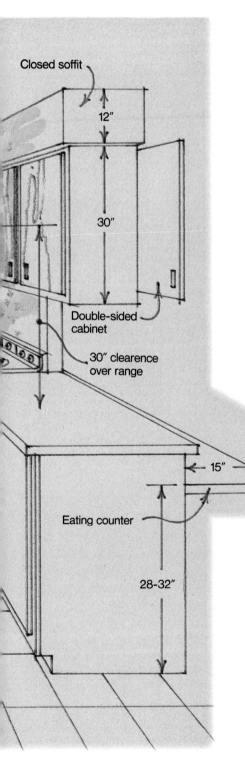

Closed soffit

12"

30"

Double-sided cabinet

30" clearence over range

15"

Eating counter

28-32"

Cabinets come in many sizes and configurations—with good reason. How far you can reach comfortably, the space required for chores, and the height and width of appliances all govern cabinet measurements. Here are the dimensions you need to do the job.

Why are countertops almost always 36" from the floor? Because that's long been considered the most comfortable worktop height for a woman, and, at least so far, kitchens have been designed primarily for use by women.

Research indicates that most women have a comfortable overhead reach of 68", the height at which you'll find the highest regularly used shelf in a wall-hung cabinet. That's also why the more frequently used upper drawers in a base cabinet are about 28" from the floor—so they can be opened without stooping.

How far the average woman can stretch her arms straight out in front of her is called "reach radius," and that determines not only the 25" standard depth of a countertop, but the depths of cabinets, too. Reach radius, plus the amount of space needed for cooking, baking, and cleanup, also decides the clearance between wall cabinets

This kitchen has many more cabinets of different dimensions than you'd find in any one kitchen. That's so you can see how different-sized cabinets can efficiently fill space. At left, full-height cabinets add storage space. At one end of the kitchen, you'll see extra-deep cabinets and counter. On the right, "standard" height cabinets used with a closed soffit.

and countertops, oven ranges, and space needed around ovens, sinks, and dishwashers.

Standard measurements and special requirements

In the drawing of the composite kitchen, left, you'll see how these and other standard measurements come into play in a room with the usual 8' ceiling. Except for the range, we omitted the appliances you'd normally find in a modern kitchen for the sake of clarity. (see appliance dimensions, *page 91*).

We've also indicated three common ways to treat soffits: (1) closed, to conceal the tops of wall cabinets; (2) open, for possible display space above cabinets; and (3) filled with full-height cabinets for additional storage.

Sometimes, standard cabinet dimensions must adapt to special circumstances. In a kitchen designed for the elderly, for example, you'd want to lower the highest functional shelf 3", raise the lowest shelf or drawer 3", and provide a work surface about 1½" lower than standard.

For the physically disabled person who must cook from a wheelchair, countertops should only be 31" from the floor. To accommodate the chair under the counter during meal preparation, you have to provide a free space 30" wide by 29½" high. This allows a full 24" of forward reach on top of the counter.

Kitchens—and cabinets—also should be tailored to how your family cooks, and the space you have to work with. If you favor lots of fresh-baked breads and pastries, think about a special area with a 30" deep countertop for rolling dough. Lots of small, labor-saving appliances, such as food processors, might require their own storage area that you'll have to custom-dimension.

continued

STANDARDS FOR KITCHEN CABINETS
continued

If you're starting from scratch with an empty room, use this rule of thumb to calculate the number of cabinets you'll need: Basic storage requires 9' of base and wall cabinets, *plus* 3' of cabinets for each member of the family regularly eating at home. A family of four requires 21 running feet of both wall and base units.

Wall cabinets: sized for versatility

Wall cabinets normally mount directly on the wall, but they can also hang from the ceiling over an island or peninsula with access from both sides. No matter how you use them, wall cabinets should be 12" deep when installed over a 25"-deep countertop, and 15" deep over a 30" countertop.

How high you make wall cabinets depends on how much storage you need. With a closed or open soffit, the standard wall cabinet height is 30", providing two shelves for three compartments within. If you want to use soffit space for storage, install 42" full-height cabinets. The different cabinet heights you'd use in open, closed, or full-height situations appear below in the cabinet illustrations.

The width of wall cabinets, usually from 9" to 36", is determined by the width of the matching base cabinets immediately below, since in most cases, the units are viewed as a pair. Whether a wall cabinet has one door or two, however, depends on its width. Doors wider than their height tend to sag because of the weight on the hinges, so wide cabinets have two doors.

Detailed dimensions of a wall

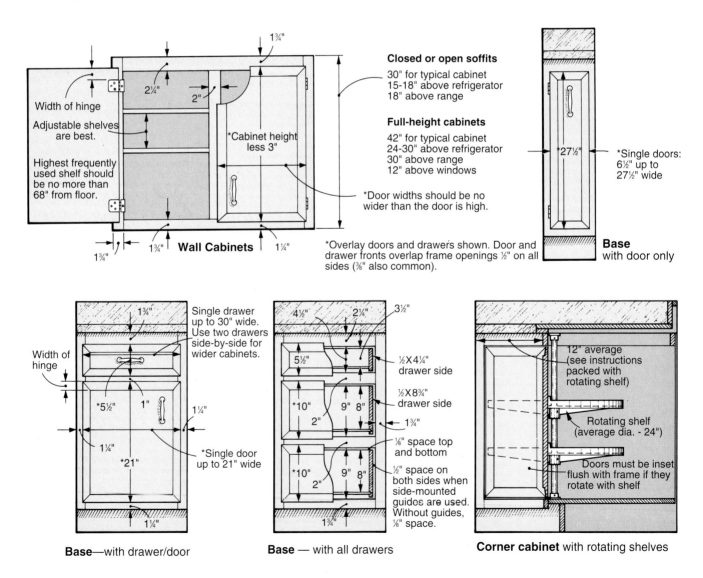

cabinet are shown in the illustration, *on the opposite page*. Use them for reference when you detail your kitchen cabinet project plans.

Base cabinets: dividing up storage space

You may want a special narrow cabinet of 9" to hold cookie sheets and trays next to the stove, or an undersink cabinet 42" wide. However, base cabinets normally measure about 24" deep and 34½" high (adding a 1½" countertop brings them up to 36"). Extra-deep base cabinets of 29" maximize countertop area for tasks such as baking, or storage for small appliances (you also can set standard-depth cabinets away from the wall and cover them with a 30" countertop). Toe kicks are 3" deep by 4" high.

Divide up the space in a base cabinet with all shelves and a door or doors, all drawers, or a combination of drawer and doors, as in the typical configurations shown *on the opposite page*. As with wall cabinets, the width of the cabinet determines whether you should use one drawer or door, or two.

Allowing for size and use of appliances

Your kitchen appliances also affect the dimensions of many of your cabinets, as well as countertop area. Luckily, appliance manufacturers heed standards, too. That's why a built-in dishwasher fits snugly under a countertop and a drop-in range scoots in with room to spare.

In the box *below* you'll find a complete chart of appliance dimensions, as well as those for single-, double-, and triple-bowl sinks. Use these as a planning guide for countertop cutouts and spacing between base cabinets, but *always refer to the specific sink or appliance model you'll use for exact installation instructions.*

Besides dimensions, you'll have to allow countertop workspace to use your appliances, as well as the sink. While your space may require adjusting these ideal situations, here are some considerations:

- Ranges, including built-in or countertop microwaves, should have about 18" of work area on either side; ovens, about 15" on one side.
- To load or unload a refrigerator, allow approximately 18" of counter on the door-opening side.
- Try to provide space on both sides of the sink for cleanup—30" to the right and 24" to the left.

Shelving, special cabinets, and eating counters

If possible, make all cabinet shelving adjustable with shelf supports or a pin system. That way, you can vary heights and spacing to meet your changing needs.

Specialized cabinets add convenience or utilize normally wasted space, such as the lazy susan corner shown on the *facing page*. You can purchase its rotating shelves as a unit to install in your handcrafted cabinet.

Other specialty cabinets include those to house microwaves and separate conventional ovens, pantries and broom closets, and units used for desks and cookbook storage. Cabinets of this type have to be customized to your space.

Eating counters range from the informal high bar to casual family seating at table height. Bar-height counters measure 42"–45" from the floor and require about 7"–9" knee space with a 30" bar stool that has a footrest. You can also build one to match your 36"–high countertop by providing a 10" knee space and using 24"-high stools. Table-height counters are 28"–32" from the floor, and require 18" of knee room and chairs 18" high.

How long should your counter be? Allow 21" of length for each person served. A 15" depth provides space for a place setting. Two diners facing each other at a table or booth need a minimum of 30" combined.

APPLIANCE AND SINK DIMENSIONS

Unless you buy commercial or European units almost all appliances fall within the following range of dimensions. Refer to them when planning your cabinets, but get actual measurements before you build.

APPLIANCE	HEIGHT	WIDTH	DEPTH
Range, floor model	35⅛ -36"	19½ -40"	24½ -26¼"
Range, w/eye-level oven	61½-67⁷⁄₁₆"	29⅞-40"	25½ -27⅝"
Range, drop-in	23-23½"	22⅞-23⁷⁄"	22⅛ -25"
Cooktop	2-3"	12 - 48"	18 - 22"
Wall oven, single	23½ -25"	21-24"	21⅛ -22¹¹⁄₁₆"
Wall oven, double	39¼-50⅜"	21-24"	21⅛ -22¹¹⁄₁₆"
Wall oven w/broiler	38-40³⁄₁₆"	21-24"	21⅛-22¹¹⁄₁₆"
Range hood	5½ -7½"	24-72"	12-27½"
Microwave	13⅝-18"	21½-22½"	14½-22"
Refrigerator	55½ -68⅞"	24-35½"	26⁹⁄₁₆-32⅞"
Dishwasher	33½-34½"	23-24¼"	23¹¹⁄₁₆ -26¼"
Trash compactor	33½-34½"	11⅞-14⅞"	18-24³⁄₁₆"

SINK	LENGTH	WIDTH
Single bowl	11½ -33"	13-22⅜"
Double bowl	28-46"	16-25"
Triple bowl	43 - 54"	22"

WOODWORKERS' STANDARDS FOR SCREWS

Specific standards govern just about every facet of woodworking, and screws are no exception to the rule. Here we present a handy reference guide to fastening with screws.

What's there to know about screws, except that you never seem to have enough of the right kind when you need them?

After talking with fastener manufacturers, professional woodworkers, and the "always-has-the-answer" man at the hardware store, we may have some surprises for you. We learned, for instance, about all the materials from which screws are made, and why you'd use one over the other; their different lengths and diameter sizes; head shapes and slot styles; and the importance of a correctly sized pilot hole.

And, if you've had it with digging through cans, jars, and bins to find just the right screws to finish your project, you'll also learn which ones you ought to keep on hand. Then, you can say good-bye to those minutes-before-closing dashes to your hardware store.

Choosing the right screw begins with the metal

Steel screws represent the least expensive and most common type available. They're strong, but like your car, they'll rust without protection. That's why steel screws normally have a shiny plating of cadmium or zinc chromate. Unplated screws start with a blue hue, but eventually oxidize to rust-brown.

When you need high strength plus corrosion resistance, opt for *stainless-steel* screws. You might have to special order them (your hardware store can do that), as well as pay double the price, but they'll

hold up in outdoor furniture and high-humidity situations.

Steel *case-hardened* screws, originally developed for the manufacture of particleboard products, prove exceptionally tough because they've been heat-tempered. Case-hardened screws have a dull, flat-black finish and a skinny shank. They're used most often with a power screwdriver for driving into hardwood and particleboard. For projects exposed to the weather, you'll want them galvanized or plated, at, of course, higher cost. And, you might have to special order them.

With case-hardened screws, you can choose from two thread styles. *Double-leads,* or "hi-lo," have twin threads and work well in hardwoods. One-thread, *single-lead* styles are best for softwoods and particleboard because they hold. (See illustration *below.*)

Brass screws can add a handsome accent when exposed, match hardware, or endure the elements. But, they're not as strong as steel and may twist off if you drive them into too small a pilot hole. Their slots will also wear if you use them in a situation where they'll be removed and reinstalled often. However, in projects calling for oak, which contains a tannic acid that reacts with ferrous metal, woodworkers normally choose brass to avoid unsightly staining.

Aluminum screws corrode quickly in contact with dissimilar metals and twist off more easily than brass if you apply too much muscle. So, they're an unlikely choice for woodworking, *except* when your project demands aluminum hardware.

Sorting out screw sizes

Compared to other materials and fasteners, screw sizes are a breeze to figure out. Their *gauge* refers to shank diameter in a range from #0 (the smallest) to #24 (the largest). Gauge increases by .013" or about 1/64", in each increment.

Screw lengths begin at 1/4" and reach 4" or longer, though you'll probably stay in the middle range in your home woodworking. To cover all possible applications, each length comes in three or more diameters. As a rule, the smaller the gauge of the screw, the thinner the wood you should use it in.

Head styles you can drive home

Just as screws of different metals work better in various materials or situations, different screw-head styles suit a divergence of woodworking needs and requirements. (See drawing *on page 93, top.*)

Choose *flathead* screws for general assembly, where you will countersink or counterbore the screw before covering with putty or plugs. When a flush surface isn't important, or when you want a decorative effect, *roundhead* screws fill the bill.

You use *oval-head* screws primarily to install hardware, such as cabinet hinges, because their shape matches the machined hole snugly.

Besides differing head styles, screws also come in choices of

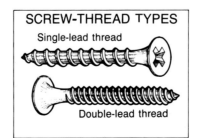

SCREW-THREAD TYPES

Single-lead thread

Double-lead thread

SCREW-HEAD TYPES

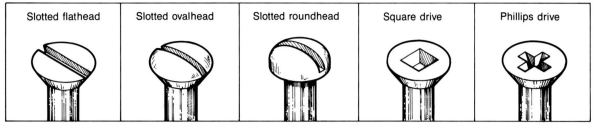

| Slotted flathead | Slotted ovalhead | Slotted roundhead | Square drive | Phillips drive |

drive slots to match your tools (again, refer to drawing, *above*).

The *straight-slot* fastens with a standard-tip or cabinetmaker's screwdriver mated to the width and thickness of the slot. This insures positive drive. A screwdriver too narrow and thin reduces torque and can mangle the slot, while one too wide mars the wood surrounding the hole and limits its drive depth.

Phillips-head screws have grown in popularity with the increasing use of the power screwdriver. With the cross-shaped slot, the driver tip self centers in the head to lessen the chance of its slipping off to damage the workpiece.

The *square-hole* or "Robertson" type screw head goes the Phillips-head one better for positive, slip-free fastening. Developed for production work, this type requires a square-tipped driver (which you can buy separately to pop into your power driver).

How to buy screws

Wood screws are generally sold by the box; those 4" and shorter packed in quantities of 100. Screws over 4" come in boxes containing 25 or 50, depending on their gauge and length. Most hardware dealers, of course, let you buy less than a box, but the individual price goes up.

If you have to order wood screws from your hardware dealer or mail-order supplier, you must specify the type of head, type of slot, length, diameter (gauge), material, and finish. The abbreviations FH, RH, and OH refer to flathead, roundhead, and ovalhead screws.

The pilot hole: tight, but not too tight

Think of a pilot hole as a custom-fitted binocular or gun case. As you can see in the drawing *below,* it grips every contour of the screw, allowing the threads to bite and hold in the wood.

Forget the widespread belief that a pilot hole has to be one size smaller than the screw—this often results in split wood. When you drill a pilot hole, you're guided by the screw's dimensions: its length, the diameter of its shank, pilot (less threads), and head (for

countersinking, or counterboring, if a plug will be used). The easiest way to accomplish this is with a *screw pilot,* which drills all parts and configurations of the hole in one operation. Real time-savers, they're available to match common screw sizes (some screw pilots are adjustable for different lengths).

Some types of case-hardened screws, designed for rapid assembly of cabinets, have special auger points that bore into the wood as they're driven in place

continued

ANATOMY OF A PILOT HOLE

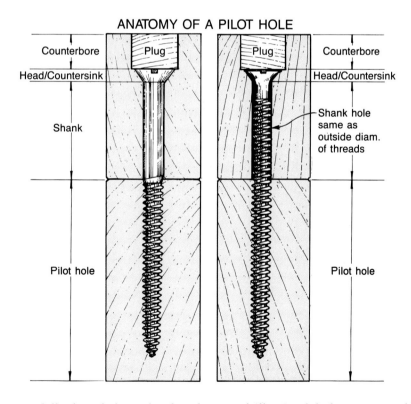

Counterbore
Plug
Head/Countersink
Shank
Pilot hole

Plug
Counterbore
Head/Countersink
Shank hole same as outside diam. of threads
Pilot hole

For a fully threaded case-hardened screw, drill a shank hole as you would for a normal screw or it won't draw up.

STANDARDS FOR SCREWS
continued

SHOP REFERENCE GUIDE (Screws shown are actual size)													
TYPICAL USES	**ATTACHING SMALL HARDWARE**					**GENERAL ASSEMBLY**			**HEAVY-DUTY ASSEMBLY**			**GENERAL ASSEMBLY W/POWER DRIVER**		
GAUGE	2	3	4	5	6	7	8	9	10	12	14	6	8	10
HEAD BORE SIZE	$11/64''$	$13/64''$	$15/64''$	$1/4''$	$9/32''$	$5/16''$	$11/32''$	$23/64''$	$25/64''$	$7/16''$	$1/2''$	$5/16''$	$11/32''$	$11/32''$
SHANK DRILL SIZE	$3/32''$	$7/64''$	$7/64''$	$1/8''$	$9/64''$	$5/32''$	$5/32''$	$11/64''$	$3/16''$	$7/32''$	$1/4''$	$1/8''$	$5/32''$	$3/16''$
PILOT DRILL SIZE	$1/16''$	$1/16''$	$5/64''$	$5/64''$	$3/32''$	$7/64''$	$7/64''$	$1/8''$	$1/8''$	$9/64''$	$5/32''$	$3/32''$	$7/64''$	$9/64''$

AVAILABLE LENGTHS—SHORTEST TO LONGEST (INCHES)

1/4, 3/8, 1/2, 5/8, 3/4, 7/8, 1, 1 1/4, 1 1/2, 1 3/4, 2, 2 1/4, 2 1/2, 2 3/4, 3, 3 1/4, 3 1/2, 3 3/4, 4

with a power screwdriver. Their tempered toughness allows them to resist twist-off, and they actually store chips in their shank as they bore (this eliminates heat buildup). Even with all their driving power, auger-point screws may still require pilot holes in end or edge grain, and that presents a hitch: To our knowledge, screw pilots aren't available to match case-hardened screws, so you have to change bits for the two-step operation. Or, use a drill bit with a countersink attached.

On using screws

Assembling a project with screws can be quick and hassle-free, if you heed this advice from our shop:

• Always lubricate screws before inserting them. Of all we've tried, beeswax works best for us.

• Drill a test hole for the size screw you intend to use. To make it smaller or larger, change bits in $\frac{1}{64}$" or $\frac{1}{32}$", not $\frac{1}{16}$", increments.

• Brass screws are naturally softer, so the pilot hole should be roomier to prevent twist-off.

• Case-hardened screws hold, but those with completely threaded shanks can't pull pieces together. To assemble with this type, you have to tightly position the pieces first.

• Keep an assortment of screws on hand. Here are some sizes for general assembly: Flathead screws in #6x1"; #8x¾", 1", 1¼", 1½", 2"; and #10x1½". Case-hardened screws in #8x1⅛" and #10x1¼", 2", and 3".

WOODWORKERS' STANDARD LAYOUT TOOLS

Draftsmen rely on specialized layout tools to produce top-quality work. In their business, it's not good enough to be "almost-on." They've got to be exact. And so do woodworkers.

The basic seven

Mechanical pencil: For precision in tracing patterns and marking cutoff lines, it's tough to beat the consistent, fine line of a mechanical pencil.

Plastic eraser: Not all erasers are created equal. Plastic erasers won't abrade paper or leave a fuzzy line behind. On wood, a plastic eraser gets into the grain without leaving a mark or residue.

French curves: These ingenious tools have nearly all the curves you'll ever need to enlarge a pattern or grid. Just transfer the pattern's grid intersection points to a larger grid, and use a French curve to connect the points. Purchase three sizes—the Alvin 351, 352, and 353 set works well—so you'll always have the radius you need.

Adjustable triangle: Because this versatile tool adjusts from 0 to 90°, it saves you the cost of buying numerous triangles, while guaranteeing accurate angle cuts every time. The Mars Staedtler 6" model is a good choice for its quality and convenient size.

Circle templates: How many times have you searched for a jar lid to draw a circle? Next time, use a circle template in combination with a mechanical pencil to get premeasured, perfectly round circles. With two of these templates, you can make any of 50 different circles from $\frac{1}{16}$ to 3".

These make drawing corner radii easy, too. If a plan calls for a 1"

radius, select the 2"-diameter circle, nestle it in a corner until two edges make contact, and draw the radius.

Protractor: Inexpensive, but handy, a protractor provides an easy and accurate way to set a sliding bevel and check other angles.

You can also use a protractor to divide a circle into segments by dividing the necessary number of parts into 360° (an entire circle). For example, plot the hours on the face of a clock by dividing 360° by 12; then mark hours every 30° around a circle.

Parallel spacer: Making parallel lines along a straight edge is simple, but this device also allows you to parallel a curve. Place your mechanical pencil in the correct hole, and you can draw a parallel line .025 to .5" ($\frac{1}{40}$ to $\frac{1}{2}$") from any edge.

Three nice-to-have tools

Compass: With a compass, you can create an infinite number of circle sizes and perform many more advanced geometric functions such as dividing an angle or drawing an ellipse. One of the available Mars Staedtler models draws circles up to 14" in diameter.

Flexible curve: You can bend these to nearly any shape up to 20" long. Because it will retain its shape, you can transfer exact curves easily by lifting the tool and moving it.

Matte acetate: Copy a pattern onto this material, as with tracing paper, and enjoy these advantages:

• Acetate is more durable and transparent than tracing paper.

• You can use acetate over and over to transfer patterns onto wood surfaces using carbon paper and a burnishing point.

ACKNOWLEDGMENTS

Writers

Jim Barrett—Get Smooth Results from Your Belt Sander, page 9

Larry Clayton—Basic Mortise and Tenon Joinery, pages 23–28

James R. Downing—Woodworkers' Standards for Tables, pages 81–83

James R. Downing with Peter J. Stephano—Drawings and Plans, pages 70–73; Woodworkers' Standards for Screws, pages 92–95

Bill Krier—How to Install Jointer Knives, pages 12–13

Bill Krier with Jim Boelling—Making and Installing Dovetailed Drawers, pages 51–56

Bill Krier with Jim Boelling and James R. Downing—Ten Winning Ways to Work with Plywood, pages 57–62; 17 Ways to Turn Your Drill Press into a Shop Hero, pages 63–69

Bill Krier with James R. Downing—Woodworkers' Standard Layout Tools, page 95

Peter J. Stephano with James R. Downing—Reproducing Project Patterns, pages 74–77; Woodworkers' Standards for Bookcases and Shelves, pages 84–87; Woodworkers' Standards for Kitchen Cabinets, pages 88–91

Photographers

Bob Calmer
Larry Clayton
John Hetherington
Hopkins Associates
James Kascoutas

Illustrators

Advertising Art Studios Inc.
Kim Downing
Randall Foshee
Mike Henry
Greg Roberts
Jim Stevenson
Bill Zaun

If you would like to order any additional copies of our books, call 1-800-678-2802 or check with your local bookstore.